Great American Wine

The Wine Rebel's Manual

With great love and admiration, I dedicate this manual to my wife Shawna and children Stephanie, Athena and Daniel.

Great American Wine

The Wine Rebel's Manual

by
Craig Renaud

with Tony and Suzanne Bamonte

Tony and Suzanne Bamonte
P.O. Box 8625
Spokane, WA 99203

Printed in the United States of America
by Walsworth Publishing and Printing Company
Marceline, Missouri 64658

Library of Congress Control Number 2006906350
ISBN–13: 978-0-9740881-6-7
ISBN–10: 0-9740881-6-1

Front cover: The Wine Rebel at the Peterson Winery, Healdsburg, California.
Back cover: *Napa Dawn* by Stephen Charles Shortridge, Coeur d'Alene, Idaho.

Tornado Creek Publications
P.O. Box 8625
Spokane, WA 99203
Phone: (509) 838-7114
Fax: (509) 455-6798

About the Author

W e first met Craig Renaud, the "Wine Rebel," in 2004. He was looking for someone to help write and publish a book that would champion the American wine industry. In researching his background, we learned he has been in the wine business for over 18 years and has probably tasted more wines than most critics in the nation. He is recognized as one of the best California wine brokers and has been among the top in sales volume.

Renaud impressed us, not only as a wine expert, but as a person. We felt what he wanted to do was unique and would be of value to anyone interested in wine. He is a genuine American wine advocate with a lot of world savvy. His core theme is his sincere conviction that the taste and quality of American wine can outclass any of the wines in the

"The Wine Rebel."

world and still be affordable to all who would enjoy wine, both for its simple pleasure and its health benefits.

Wine plays a role in nearly every type of celebration and is an expression of romance, good fortune and success. However, today there is often so much pretentious protocol surrounding the selection and enjoyment of wine that many people feel intimidated by it. Renaud understands this and pokes fun at what he feels is smoke-and-mirrors in the wine industry. He also touches on some of life's great little secrets often admired in many successful and respected people, such as the importance of simple etiquette and common courtesy. This manual is certain to both entertain and educate! Novice and the connoisseur alike will enjoy his unique approach to the world's most revered and ancient drink as well as his little tips for a better life.

Renaud has strong family values. He is married with three children, two girls and a boy. When asked to place his priorities, he puts God and family first, but feels the challenge and successes of satisfying his wine customers are among his greatest pleasures.

It has been an honor and a learning experience to work with the Wine Rebel in bringing his long-held dream to fruition.

Tony and Suzanne Bamonte, writers and publishers

Acknowledgments

We are deeply appreciative of the various editorial contributions provided by Lorna Aites, Laura Arksey, Albert Clark, Evelyn Conant, Celia Emmerich, John Leshinski, Jeff Libarle, Tom McArthur, Dave Nelson, Randy Ouzts, Emily Sue Pike, Rick Raffaini, Karlene Rebich, John and Diane Redal, Shawna Renaud and Doris Woodward.

We also thank the following for their various contributions and involvements, which we feel helped to make this book complete: Lou Bamonte, Russ Beck, Chris Biagi, Chris and Jake Bilbro, Rob and Amy Bloem, Mark Blumhagen, Perry Boaz, Jim Bolser, Tom Boyer, William and Marcia Bond, Robin Briley, Dr. Paul Brillhart, Angelo and Julie Brunson, Gary and Cleo Clizer, Jennifer Compau, Eric Cook, Dave Culley, Nilol Dedischew, Frankie Dietz, Rob Elder, Josh Edmondson, Ryan Evans, Steve Funk, Patrick Glazer, Frank Harty, Brad Hathaway, Chris ☐Youngblood☐Hendry, Jim and Ruth Knepshield, Andy Magnus, Sean and Charissa McCoy, Chris Mueller, Tim Newcomb, Dean Opsal, Angelia (Watson) Palm, Fred Peterson, Lisa Prowe, Bob and Arlene Quintin, Silda Pollard, Dennis and Dawna Reed, Athena Renaud, Daniel Renaud, Stephanie Renaud, Skip Robinett, Dawne Sacchetti, Ally Schaeffer, Barbara Schaeffer, Stephen and Cathy Shortridge, Troy and Sidney Sylte, Stretch Strachan, Alex Smith, Nate Smith, Jonathan and Shelly Stone, Nikesha Thompson, Gene Tillman and Ben Whitney.

Introduction

Chapter 1

Challenging the Condescending, Trendy, Scheming Wine-Rating System: Page 11

A short study of the wine grading system as it applies to the integrity of marketing wines.

Chapter 2

Foreign Relations: The Balance Between the Importing and Exporting of Wine: Page 21

Looking at import statistics of foreign wines into the United States and the influence of the world's most powerful wine critic on those statistics.

Chapter 3

Support Your American Wine Industry: Page 28

Why we should support our American wine industry – patriotism and quality of product. Where America is headed in the wine industry.

Chapter 4
Your Friend the Wine Broker: Page 31
The role a wine broker plays in the competitive world of wine. Secrets for finding great wines and the advantages of using a wine broker.

Chapter 5
Having Fun with Robert Parker:
How to Distinguish Various Percentages of Truth
in Wine Terminology Within 10 Seconds or Less: Page 37
A look at many of the contemporary wine descriptions and their purposes. Having fun with the world-famous wine critic, Robert Parker. This chapter will expose you to some of the world's greatest "wine bull."

Chapter 6
Drinking Wine for Health Reasons: Page 47
Information about wine and longevity. The French Paradox. Exploring the healthy elements in wine. The Mediterranean Diet and a simple guide to good living.

Chapter 7
Etiquette: The Key to Success and Happiness: Page 55
Rewards of polite and considerate behavior. Wine tasting protocol in restaurants. How to amaze your friends and order wine in a classy restaurant. Sommelier versus wine steward. Serving wine at home. American dining etiquette. The language of flowers.

Chapter 8
Memorable Wine Drinking Destinations
From High to Low Places – A Glimpse of the West: Page 77
A pictorial tour and introduction to favorite and interesting locations throughout parts of America's Inland Northwest.

Chapter 9
Wine Myths and Misconceptions: Page 123
Exploring some of the world's most common and interesting wine myths.

Chapter 10
A Brief History of Wine From the Ancient
Egypt to the New World: Page 132
The history of wine as it applies to Egypt, the Greeks and Romans, Bacchus, the Bible, the Middle Ages, Northern Europe, the British Isles and the New World.

Chapter 11

Great American Wine Country: Page 143

The beginning of the wine industry in America. The major wine producing states. California's wine queens and a profile of the 1961 National Wine Queen.

Chapter 12

Prohibition, Temperance and Art Depicting the Evils of Drinking Alcoholic Beverages To Excess: Page 159

Circumstances that led up to the temperance movement and subsequent prohibition. The emotions of both in the artwork of the era.

Chapter 13

Wine in Art: Page 165

Some of the world's most famous wine-related artwork by the masters.

Chapter 14

How to Drink Wine and Still Go to Heaven: Page 178

A brief study of five of the world's largest and best known religions, and their positions on alcohol.

Chapter 15

Bounty of the Harvest – Types of Grapes and Wine: Page 191

Renaud's mythical goddess of the American wine vat. Basic and most common wine varietals. The vineyard and grape production. Wine facts and measurements.

Chapter 16

Making Wine: The Art and Science: Page 199

Narrative and photos of the entire wine producing process, from picking grapes to bottling wine.

Glossary of Common Wine Terms: Page 216

Index: Page 219

Introduction

Wine is my business and has been for almost two decades. I'm a wine broker specializing in American wines, especially those of the West. My job is to find, recommend and sell unique fine domestic wines to my clientele nationwide by phone or on-line. I must also be able to match my customers' tastes in wine with what the market offers. I primarily represent hundreds of micro wineries. Most of the wines I sell are relatively unknown to the public, but they are among the best in the world. I also, on occasion, serve as a wine consultant to hotels and restaurants.

As a wine broker, it has been and is my job to assess and rate wines. To me, great wine, quite simply, is the essence of nature. It is sunshine, rain, exceptional locations, soil and harvests coming together to produce a beverage that, in sensible moderation, can enhance health and good will. A great wine is one that possesses all the elements passed down from the master wine makers of the world. However, what makes a great wine rests with each individual taste. My task is to match individual tastes to quality wines. The purpose of my book is to restore useful common sense to the evaluation, romance and significance of wine.

The "Wine Rebel" Craig Renaud with his wife Shawna (in white) and some friends at a wine event on the mezzanine at the legendary Davenport Hotel in Spokane, Washington. The others are from left to right: Barbara Schaeffer, Jennifer Compau and Dawna Reed.

Chapter 1

Challenging the Condescending, Trendy, Misleading Wine-Rating System

When I first entered the wine business, my goal was to excel in the profession: I wanted to know everything I could about wine and to be the best broker and wine expert I could be. A big part of my job was to match the tastes of my customers with the best wines possible – great tasting and quality wines at fair prices.

At first, like most other people in the wine industry, I felt compelled to follow the internationally accepted system for grading wine (the 100-point grading system put into use by Robert Parker in the late 1970s). However, this system was very subjective to one person's taste – Robert Parker's. His 100-point system gives the illusion of scientific objectivity to what, in my view, is essentially a subjective art. It isn't applicable or fair to the majority of sellers and consumers in America. I was also uncomfortable with Parker's preference for foreign over American wines, with no defensible basis for this partiality.

In the early stages of my wine business, I became aware of the descriptions of wines that accompanied the ratings of Robert Parker, who had become the world's most powerful wine critic. I began to take note of the elaborate, somewhat colorful verbiage that appears in his journal, the *Wine Advocate*. Out of curiosity, I tasted many of the wines he described, but wasn't able to detect the same flavors. I soon became wary of his ratings. I felt they created a biased impact unfavorable to the American wine industry. Parker's 100-point scale denotes that wine can be measured precisely to a one-percentage point, which isn't reasonable in evaluations involving such subjective elements as taste and smell.

Wine can be measured in straightforward absolutes, such as exquisite, great, good, okay or bad, which is basically how a good wine critic should score. However, in the end, a wine critic's job is to guide consumers to the good years and vintages of wines. The selected wine will simply be either exquisite, great, good, okay or bad, based on the tastes of the individual.

In my opinion, price is typically the major, and often only, difference between great or good wine scores by Parker versus great or good wine scored by some of America's best wine critics. Truly great wines don't have to sell for outrageous prices and only do so because of the various exaggerated hypes used to promote them and the willingness of the gullible to buy them.

To better understand my perspective regarding the wine scoring system, I am going to provide a brief background of Robert Parker, when and how he got into the business, and how he became successful. Robert Parker, a native of Baltimore, was a practicing attorney for the first decade of his active career, rising to the post of assistant general counsel for the Farm Credit Banks of Baltimore. With no prior experience in the wine field, he rose to fame in the late 1970s when he began publishing his monthly journal, the *Wine Advocate,* which was an independent consumer guide to wine. Today, this publication is generally considered the world's most influential wine magazine, and possibly is the largest in circulation. Parker appears to favor the French market and, in 1999, he was awarded France's highest honor – the Chevalier of the Order of the Legion of Honor.

In the *Wine Advocate,* Parker began using the 100-point system for scoring wine. His opinion has such tremendous worldwide influence that a great number of vintners purposely strive to satisfy his palette. It is disconcerting that a majority of the sophisticated wine-consuming public has allowed one man to have such a great influence that impacts the livelihood of many individuals. A number of other wine critics have begun to parrot his misleading rhetoric.

I've read many of the descriptions of tastes and aromas he has used to support various ratings. The following is a sampling of Parker's wine descriptions:

> ...lead pencil, oily tannin, jammy black cherries, upfront charm, distinctive mineral, compost, mushrooms, melted road tar, oily tangerine like, truffle infused black cherries, aromas of ink, graphite, burnt tar, iron, scorched earth, melted licorice, spice box, tobacco leaf, creosote, dried provincial herbs, smoky licorice, graphite, charcoal, loamy soil, buttered popcorn, chocolate covered pears, gravel, stones, peppered black cherry, pit fruits, talcum powder aromas, stone aromas, liquid aromas, and liquid minerals...

I've tasted thousands of different wines, but have never tasted underbrush, gravel, stones, or many of Parker's other descriptions, in any wine. I basically haven't recognized many of the elements Parker seems to detect in wine. It appears much of what he verbally passes as his wine expertise is simply nonsense.

Is there any real objectivity in Parker's 100-point scale? Typically, a score is a test, assessment or grade. When grading on a scale of one to 100, you think of a test that has 100 questions with one point given for each question; or 50 questions with two points, or 25 questions with four points, etc. If you have a test with 100 questions and you answer 25 wrong, your grade is 75. How can this work for wine when there is no way to account for each point? How can you determine an absolute measurement in tasting wine? What's the difference between a Parker-scored 84 or an 86?

Cartoon designed by Tim Newcomb for this publication.

One of the first things I realized when I tried to apply Parker's rating system was that it is virtually impossible to rate a wine on a 100-point scale. Conduct your own test, or even just imagine it. Line up 10 different bottles of recognized quality wine with the labels removed, or even better, to be perfectly on target with this grading system, line up 100 different bottles of quality wine. Be sure you don't know the price or recognize the bottles. Taste each wine and then grade each with a number. Remember these are all quality wines, so grade them with a number between 85 and 100. You won't proceed far into your grading before getting pretty confused. Imagine! Is this an 85 or an 86 or a 90? If you did manage to grade these wines, have someone rearrange them and grade them again the following day. Do you think you will come up with the same scores? On a scale of 100, how can anyone possibly fine-tune the taste of a wine to 85 or 86. In addition to this, the test does not take into consideration that no two peoples' tastes are exactly the same.

The overwhelming majority of American wines are not rated; however, many are excellent wines and just as good as rated wines. I'm troubled that one man's taste can create a $300-plus bottle of wine from a $50 bottle. It would be interesting to see a blind wine test performed on some of Parker's 95-scored wines versus some of his 85s. Or pit some of his recommended $500 French wines against some of America's $40 or $50 wines.

A typical American wine tasting event in northern Idaho. Interestingly, these judges are committing a rather serious faux pas – they are not holding their glasses by the stems. Refer to etiquette chapter in this book.

In addition to being an art, the production of wine is a science based on scientific principles. If quality ingredients (grapes, soil and climate) are present and the proper procedures are followed for the type of wine desired, the result will be good to perfect wines.

Every person's taste is unique. Wine, which is a beverage dependent on keenly subjective judgments, should not rely on a system of numeric scores or one person's opinion, to succeed in the marketplace.

The judging of wine by numeric scores is strongly defended by those who reap the benefits of those scores. How many wine marketers would advertise their wines in a magazine that gives them a low rating? A full-page ad in any national magazine is priced in the thousands of dollars. How many of the smaller vintners can afford these ads? In fairness to the entire wine industry, wine should be evaluated in a manner based on the integrity of the wine, the scorer and each consumer's individual preference.

With thousands of good foreign and domestic wines, consumers want some kind of guidance. When wine reviewers assess wines, they basically consider taste, color, smell, and sometimes, unfortunately, politics. Other than that, no two people will taste wine exactly the same way. Further, each reviewer has his or her preferences. Consequently, as a wine broker, I must learn my customers' tastes and match wine to those tastes. However, as I stated earlier, my general approach to grading wine is simple: exquisite, great, good, okay or bad. This system could also work well using five stars.

The same panel of judges as in the earlier photo, but in a more formal setting. Note in this photo the judge on the right is smoking while tasting. This is normally frowned upon.

Rating Wine
the Wine Rebel's Way

The Wine Rebel briefing the judges at the 10th annual Wine, Stein and Dine 2006 benefit held at the Greyhound Park & Convention Center in Post Falls, Idaho. Prior to scoring the wines, each judge was given a handout explaining the five-star scoring system and why it's recommended.

One of the most important concepts I try to make when briefing judges prior to a wine judging event is the actual ease of the scoring. Each judge is given two documents I designed specifically for these types of events: *Realism in Wine Descriptions* and *Scoring Sheet for Blind Wine Testing.*

My first handout, *Realism in Wine Descriptions*, clearly illustrates the absurdity of the 100-point method which is used to exploit people who buy expensive wines for show. Following a 15-minute reading and briefing with the judges, I present them with the second handout, my simply-designed, self-explanatory scoring sheet. It is illustrated and described on the following page.

Based on common sense and the average wine connoisseur's taste, the highest quality and best tasting wines can be easily identified. In other words, I can take a random sample of people who enjoy and recognize good wine and, if given a good selection of wines to choose from, with the five-star rating system, we can compete with any of the world's experts.

Scoring Sheet for Blind Wine Testing

Date_____Event_____

Appearance: Your personal appreciation of the color.
Aroma: Your appreciation of the smell.
Body: Texture - feel in the mouth
Taste: Base this on balance and personal satisfaction of the flavors you detect.
Finish: Lingering of flavors after swallowing and aftertaste.

Exquisite	★★★★★
Great	★★★★
Good	★★★
Okay	★★
Bad	

Give from one to five points for each category, one being the lowest and five being the highest. **To obtain the final score for each wine add all points across the column and divide by five – then round off to highest number. Convert final numbers to stars.**

Wine Varietal	Appearance	Aroma	Body	Taste	Finish	Score	Final Scores
(Sample scoring)	2	3	2	4	3	2.8 = 3 points =	3 stars
1.							
2.							
3.							
4.							
5.							
6.							
7.							
8.							
9.							
10.							

This simple scoring sheet for blind wine testing is based on five main elements that should be considered when scoring wine. The most important emphasis for scoring is that wine is about taste. Typically, when you gather a group of experienced wine lovers together and perform blind wine testing, you will generally get a consensus of what is exquisite, great, good, okay or bad. Wine actually isn't much different than any other beverage in that way. If someone likes and has tasted many wines, it's fairly easy to select exquisite and great.

The Wine Rebel and wine tasting judges for the 10th annual Wine, Stein and Dine 2006 benefit at the Greyhound Park & Convention Center in Post Falls, Idaho. (Inset, the Wine, Stein and Dine 2006 logo.)

Dean Opsal, far left, holds the world record for Champagne Sabering. Sabering is the art of cutting off the top of a champagne bottle with a sword. It originated from the days of Napoleon when his soldiers would chop off the top of the bottle to celebrate victory in battle. Opsal established the record by successfully slicing off the tops of 20 champagne bottles in one minute. This is done without shattering the glass, leaving the contents safe to drink. To the right are the Wine Rebel and Derek Cleveland, who is the top "Ultimate Fighter" promoter and ranks among the top ultimate fight trainers in the Northwest.

Chapter 2

Foreign Relations: The Balance Between Importing and Exporting Wine

If the occasion ever arises to visit with someone who has traveled to the beautiful countryside or cities of France and, while there, spent some time wining and dining in any French town or city, ask the question: "Did you ever see any American wines on a French restaurant wine list?" The answer will probably be no. However, almost any fine restaurant in America will typically have a wine menu with a wide-ranging choice of French wines.

There seems to be an obvious lack of reciprocity between what France exports to, and what it imports from, the United States. There are probably a number of reasons for this, but I suspect the fact that America is much younger than the European nations may have something to do with it. Wine was being imported to the United States almost 200 years before the American wine industry began making its mark. I think another reason may be that the French feel, because they have been in the business much longer than the United States, their wine is superior. It's also expensive for France to import American wines, especially since the French have so many of their own wines they can sell at lower cost. They also seem to be more loyal to their country's industries than we are in America. Finally, after listening to a number of American travelers who have spent time in France, many French people just don't like Americans. According to some of my own personal experiences, I think this dislike of Americans could be the greater reason.

One of my main objectives for this manual is an attempt to introduce the common sense aspects of wine appreciation to the general American public. However, my most important goal is to promote the American wine industry and patriotism.

In the previous chapter, I talked briefly about Robert Parker and his 100-point wine-grading system. At this point, I want to further address Parker's influence on the wine industry at a worldwide level. Without a doubt, Parker is the number one world-renowned

"I'M SURE YOU HAVE LOTS OF GREAT AMERICAN WINE TO UNLOAD HERE, BUT WHAT CAN I DO, MONSIEUR? THIS IS A ONE-WAY STREET!"

wine critic. This fact is readily acknowledged and accepted by the majority of those involved in the wine industry and also proclaimed by Parker himself! My concern and disappointment with Mr. Parker, and his influence over the world's wine industry, is his ability to turn such a large number of wine drinkers into lemmings, blindly following his 100-point rating system, which creates an illusion of scientific precision. However, my main unease over Parker's influence is his apathy toward our accomplished and great American wine industry.

What the French Think of Robert Parker

On March 29, 1999, President Jacques Chirac signed a decree authorizing Robert M. Parker Jr. to be a *Chevalier dans I'Ordre de la Legion d'Honneur.* President Chirac personally decorated him at a ceremony at the Elysee Palace on June 22, 1999.

While bestowing France's highest honor, President Chirac stated: "Robert Parker is the most followed and influential critic of French wines in the world."

In 1993, the late President Francois Mitterand made Robert Parker a *Chevalier dans I'Ordre National du Merite.* The Legion of Honor was created by Napoleon Bonaparte in 1802 to honor the highest level of achievement made on the behalf of France. Robert Parker is one of only a handful of foreigners to have received France's two highest Presidential honors.

In 1993, Parker received the Wine and Vine Communication Award from Moet-Hennessey for his French language editions of Bordeaux and Burgundy. In 1995, Parker was made the third honorary citizen of the Rhone Valley's most important wine village, Chateauneuf du Pape.

On the other hand, it is interesting to note that one of the lowest scores Parker ever gave (a 56) during his wine critic career, was to a California wine, which he stated "had an intense vegetative, barnyard aroma and very unusual flavors."

The Incredible Universal Wine God

23

What Robert Parker Thinks of Himself

In July of 2003, *Wine International* magazine published an interview with Robert Parker by Panos Kakaviatos, an independent journalist, based in both France and the United States. Kakaviatos writes on wine for both *Agence France Press* and the Bordeaux-based French website *Wine Citizen*.

The Incredible Universal Wine God

The recap of Kakaviatos's interview consisted of eight typewritten pages, the crux of which consisted of Parker talking about French wines, his allegiance to France and his style as a critic.

While reading this interview, I came across one paragraph which typically sums up Parker's allegiance to France and his blatant self-importance. In this interview, Parker states:

...in the history of wine criticism or wine journalism, there has never been any critic of my stature, with a worldwide reputation and worldwide influence, that has been as pro-French as I have and that has been as much a defender of French terroir as I have.

Two paragraphs later, Parker concludes with "... I have been a tremendous defender of French wine."

The following page lists 16 of Parker's top 100 wine choices for 2003. The majority of wines on Parker's list are from France and Australia. There are only 19 American wines listed in his top 100 choices, none of which are in the top 20.

Parker's allegiance to French wines is very disturbing. In the wine world, the industry's leading critic is an American. Why doesn't he give equal attention to his own country's wines? The USA has bountiful choices of great wines that could easily be promoted and, in all fairness, should be.

Perfect 100 Scored Wines

- BULLER NV Calliope Rare Muscat
- LA CLUSIERE 2000 St. Emilion
- CHAPOUTIER 2000 White Hermitage Cuvee de L'oree
- LA MISSION HAUT BRION 2000 Pessac-Leognan
- Ch. PAVIE 2000 St. Emilion
- Ch. LAFITE-ROTHSCHILD 2000 Pauillac
- GUIGAL 1999 Cote-Rotie La Landonne
- GUIGAL 1999 Cote-Rotie La Mouline
- GUIGAL 1999 Cote-Rotie La Turque
- CH. MARGAUX 2000 Margaux
- CH. LAFLEUR 2000 Pomerol
- CHAPOUTIER 2000 White Hermitage L'Ermite
- CHAMBERS ROSEWOOD NV Rare Muskatelle
- CHAMBERS ROSEWOOD NV Rare Muscat
- CH. AUSONE 2000 St. Emilion
- CH. Petrus 2000 Pomerol

From Robert Parker's Top 100 Wines List for 2003

The above list contains the first 16 of 100 wines Robert Parker scored as his top choices. To each of these he gave scores of 100. Thirteen of these 16 wines were from France, the other three were from Australia. His total list of 100 wines contained 19 American wines, none of which were in the top 20.

America's French Wine Connection

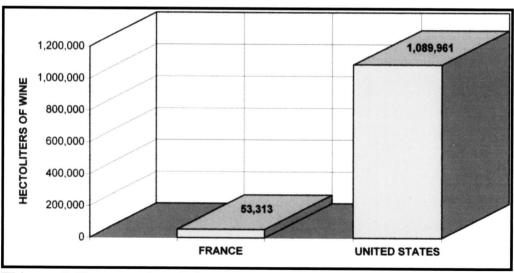

This graph illustrates the relationship of wine France imported from the United States in 2001 versus the amount the United States imported from France that same year. (This was the most recent information I was able to obtain, but it reflects the traditional trade imbalance.)

Early Evidence of the American Wine Industry's Concern for the French/U.S Trade Imbalance

This print titled *American Triumph* was an advertisement for A. Marschall & Co.'s American extra dry champagne. It was designed by the National Bureau of Engraving of Philadelphia in the 1880s.

This advertisement for American champagne depicts a radiant "Columbia" drinking American champagne, while a scowling, older French woman (on the left) carrying champagne labeled Rheims departs for a French ship in the harbor. (Rheims is a famous French champagne named for the capital city of the Champagne region, where most of the kings of France were crowned.)

Before the Statue of Liberty dominated New York Harbor, images of women were already widely used to symbolize the traits, virtues and opportunities of early America. Columbia, who emerged as an icon for the United States, was one of these symbols, and often was considered the feminine counterpart to Christopher Columbus. She was typically clothed in classical robes, often accompanied by a liberty cap and pole, with the stars and stripes of America on her shawl, dress or cap. *(Archival drawing, Library of Congress)*

Chapter 3

Support Your
American Wine Industry

S ince the declaration of America's independence in 1776, we have evolved into the greatest nation on earth. By we, I mean every race, creed and nationality that today make up our country. We, as a people, came from every country on the planet and each has brought something from their culture with them, but we now have one thing in common – we are Americans. As Americans, we have proven that anything other countries can do, we can do at least as well, if not better. We should support our country and all that defines it, which unquestionably includes the American wine industry.

Great American Wines

The French have a certain snobbish arrogance toward American wine. However, in the realm of a worldwide understanding of grapes, wine, geographical location, soil, science, skill and technology, it is pretty hard to discern any real differences among the best wines of both countries. This is especially true if you eliminate all possible sources of bias from the testing process. Supposedly the major purpose of independent wine tasting is to test if common preconceptions are really correct. To accomplish this, any information reflecting the opinions of others must be kept from influencing those making the tests. Consequently, the only fair way to judge wine is for the testers to have no knowledge of whose wine they are tasting, or where it came from. It is an established fact that blind wine tasting tests are highly resisted among wine connoisseurs. To better understand why, consider the following results of a most significant blind wine test, an event in the summer of 1976 that shook the wine world. It centered around a blind wine tasting test held in Paris, later referred to as the Judgment of Paris. Nine French experts, who were prominent in wine and food circles, painstakingly selected the best white and red wines from a selection of both French and American wines. At the conclusion of the test, the French wine jury was shocked to learn they had chosen an American Chateau Montelena Chardonnay (white) and an American Stag's Leap Wine Cellars Cabernet Sauvignon (red) as their best wines.

Let's explore the Judgment of Paris further. Here are some brief partial quotes from three of the nation's leading publications written at the time:

Time – June 7, 1976
"Judgment of Paris"

Last week in Paris, at a formal wine tasting organized by Spurrier, the unthinkable happened: California defeated all Gaul. ...

... As they swirled, sniffed, sipped and spat, some judges were instantly able to separate an imported upstart from an aristocrat. More often, the panel was confused. "Ah, back to France!" exclaimed Oliver after sipping a 1972 Chardonnay from the Napa Valley. "That is definitely California. It has no nose," said another judge – after downing a Batard Montrachet '73. Other comments included such Gallic gems as "this is nervous and agreeable," "a good nose, but not too much in the mouth," and "this soars out of the ordinary."

The New York Times – June 9, 1976
"California Labels Outdo French in Blind Test"
in Frank J. Prial's Wine Talk column

Several California white wines triumphed over some of the best Burgundy has to offer in a blind tasting in Paris recently. More startling: The judges were French ... Each judge was asked to evaluate the wines as to color, bouquet, palate and balance and to give each a numerical rating on a scale of 20 possible points. The results: Chateau Montelena, [Napa Valley] 132; Meursault - Charmes, 126.5; Chalone Vineyards, [Napa Valley] 121; Spring Mountain, [California 104]; Beaune Clos des Mouches, 101; Freemark Abbey, [Napa Valley],100; Batard Montrachet 94; Puligny-Montrachet, 89; Veedercrest Vineyards, [Napa Valley]88; and David Bruce, [California] 63 ...

The Washington Post – June 13, 1976
"Those Winning American Wines"
by William Rice

The latest in the continuing, if rather pointless, taste-offs pitting American versus French wines saw the Americans winning on France's home court ...

Never in the history of the world, has there been as much wine available to as many people as there is today. I'm going to share one of the best kept secrets I have discovered during my tenure in the wine business. Many people are regularly spending up to $200 on wine when an equivalent could easily cost $50, and the only basic difference is the label. What should all this tell you? Well, if Americans can invent the light bulb, telephone, airplane, rocket, television, computer, heart-lung machine, atomic bomb, nuclear submarine, artificial heart, build the Panama Canal saving 8,000 miles in ocean travel from the east to west coast, send men to the moon, invent the birth control pill and Viagra, they can easily make the best wine in the world – and, in fact, they do!

All the United States needs is a chance on a fair playing field to prove to the world the quality of wines our vintners can produce. This happened in 1976 and, to the best of my knowledge, it hadn't been allowed to happen again – until this year (2006). Blind wine testing of American pitted against French is rare because, generally, those in the business of promoting and selling French wines haven't wanted to risk this embarrassment again. However, the test of 1976 was recreated in 2006 to determine how well the American wines held up over these past 30 years. To the complete surprise of the French, who were quite certain the aged French wines would outshine the American wines, the top five selections were American! They prevailed over the Bordeaux wines, which are famously long-lived wines. The most remarkable part is these wines were made and bottled during a period when the California wine industry was still young and was much less developed than it is today. Of the wines, the first place winner (a 1971 Ridge Vineyards Monte Bello from the Santa Cruz Mountains) had been number five in 1976, and second place had been number one (a 1973 Stag's Leap Wine Cellars Cabernet Sauvignon from the Napa Valley). Imagine what the results would be pitting current vintages that have had the benefit of 30 years of development against the French. I'm quite certain what the outcome would be!

Chapter 4

Your Friend
the Wine Broker

The Big Wine Picture

Since the first known production of wine over 8,000 years ago, there have been an immeasurable number of various wine producers. According to ancient writings regarding the flavors of wine, most early wines were fairly basic and similar in taste, thus making wine selection fairly simple. The choices were primarily in the color and whether or not the wine had turned to vinegar. As the world's population has increased, the wine industry has grown and evolved. Over time the production of wine has become a tremendously competitive worldwide commercial industry. The quality and tastes of wine have drastically changed both in terms of the vast number of choices and in sophistication, thus making the use of an experienced wine broker a direct route to the best wine purchases for your money. An experienced wine broker's main expertise is finding both lesser and well-known, but great, wines at affordable prices.

To comprehend the degree of competition in the wine industry, consider the world's population explosion. Today the worldwide census is greater than any other time known to man. Although it would be impossible to determine an accurate count over many thousands of years, there has been enough written historical information to arrive at a rough estimate. In 10,000 BC, the entire world population was estimated to be four million. As of this writing, according to the United States Bureau of the Census, that number is now over six billion. These figures are staggering when applied to the wine industry, which has reached major production proportions in numerous nations, especially in America. Consequently, there is far too much competition in the wine industry for the wine consumer not to have the best wine at a reasonable price. One area of concern for the United States is the number of foreign countries that are making and selling wines at prices deliberately designed to undercut and capture what they can of our market. However, when given a choice of comparable wines within the same price range, the patriotic consumer typically selects American.

My wine interests and business are strictly American. I ride a Harley-Davidson motor-cycle, drink American wine and would die for my country. I feel I live in the greatest nation with the best wines in the world, which are only going to get better.

According to the organizer of the Bordeaux, France, wine fair, Vinexpo, America is expected to become the world's largest wine consumer, in terms of both volume and value, by 2008. In an information release, Vinexpo marketing experts asserted that by 2008, wine drinkers in the United States will account for 25 percent of all the wine bought and consumed in the world. Currently, U.S. consumers account for 19 percent. This will put the United States ahead of France, Italy and Spain. That isn't bad, considering the total population in the United States in 2005 is about 296 million. In other words, by 2008 about 5% of the entire world population will be drinking about 25% of all the wine produced in the world. Imagine the impact on our wine industry if we all supported American wines, and why not? As you will see later in this manual, I feel we produce the best wines in the world.

Why is America headed toward that distinction? Americans are producing great wines, and the public is becoming educated on the health benefits. For centuries, wine has been the beverage of choice for families in most European countries. Wine's reputation is of candlelight and romance. Songs and poems tout wine as one of life's sophisticated pleasures. With each new bottle of wine comes the surprise and pleasure of its unique taste, the aged essence of nature's beloved and healthy fruit, the grape turned to wine. There is a pleasant secret, and often new revelation, from each bottle opened. Wine is *the* beverage for a romantic evening, for dinner with friends, soft lights, snowy evenings, sitting by a fireplace. It is near the top of life's comforts – candlelight, wine, music, flowers and those dear to us go well together. With those thoughts in mind, we know a great number of Americans will always be wine drinkers in search of that perfect wine.

The Good Fortune of the Perfect Wine

When I first entered the business, I was always on a mission with an objective to find the perfect wine. The main obstacles I encountered were the thousands of choices available and the overstated quality of many mediocre wines. However, the biggest problem was trying to purchase highly rated wines – wines with the high Robert Parker scores, or for that matter, any wines that had been graded with high scores by a prominent critic. They just weren't easily available. Typically, by the time you read about an alleged great, high-scored wine in the *Wine Spectator* or almost any wine publication that scores wine, they aren't available – the wine "insiders" have already purchased them for astronomically inflated prices, based solely on the scores.

I refer to these highly scored wines as "trophy wines," or good wines that have been over-priced and become scarce based on some influential critic's high rating. During my years in the wine business, I have tasted thousands of various wines, including numerous wines that have received high scores from popular critics. Many of these were good, but not great, wines. They became "great" because some critic scored them high, creating a stampede for their much-sought-after-boasting-rights ownership. In reality, these trophy wines take on an almost human persona. Successful wines are just like successful people. There are hundreds of thousands of extremely brilliant and talented people, each equal to the other. What determines the success of one great person over the other is being at the right place at the right time, doing the right thing and knowing the right people, just like wines.

It will always be human nature to put "you and yours" in the best light. We all have the natural instinct to look out for ourselves. The producer of a wine is always going to boast of its quality in order to get the highest dollar, or even just be able to sell it for that matter. Any winery fortunate enough to gain a good working relationship with an important wine critic is almost guaranteed some level of success. No doubt, the majority of the wines receiving good ratings are good wines and the wineries they come from work hard to have them presented as such, but there many more wines just as good and often better that never receive ratings.

Beauty and romance is expressed in this simple wine setting.

Unfortunately, there is limited room at the top when it comes to wine or people; as an example, look at presidents of great countries, or members of Congress or CEOs of Fortune 500 companies. Often, we see incompetent or self-serving decisions being made at the upper level and we wonder how, with so much talent in the world, some of these people advanced to those top positions. Again, it's all contingent on being at the right place at the right time, doing the right thing and knowing the right people.

There are hundreds of great wineries in the United States and thousands of wines from which to choose. All things being equal in the wine producing industry (and that is the case with a substantial number of wineries), great wines are far more prevalent than wine critics would have you believe. More often than not, you could take a wine that carries a high rating, is advertised as such, priced at $200, and match it in a blind contest with a $35 to $60 bottle of my choosing. Most likely the judges would have a hard time telling the two apart, with the unrated wine standing a good chance of winning.

Being in the business and aware of the frequently misleading elite standards imposed on underperforming wines, I have found that too many consumers tend to judge wine by its price, rather than its actual quality. Ernest Gallo, for years the undisputed top wine producer in the United States, has been attributed with publicly stating that at one time he offered a buyer the same wine twice during a blind tasting, advising that the second wine was twice as expensive. The buyer chose to purchase the most expensive. I know this to be true, because on occasion, I have performed that same experiment with the same results. Too often, consumers tend to buy status wines over lesser known wines with equal or better quality.

The Advantages of a Wine Broker

• A wine broker receives and tastes new wines on a daily basis from various cutting-edge wineries, including hundreds of small wineries that strive for, and attain, perfection. Most will never be rated except by the consumer or your personal wine broker, who can match wines to your individual tastes.

• A wine broker will typically introduce new wines to his customer base long before they have become known. In the case of Parker's or other rated wines, they often won't be available for purchase in most wine outlets or not affordable by the general public.

• A wine broker offers the convenience of shipping cases of wine directly to your home or office. He will also recommend wines to match your palate.

• An experienced wine broker will, on a continuing basis, introduce you to new wines and wineries long before the critics discover them.

• Depending on who you use, a wine broker will guarantee what they sell you. If there is something wrong with the wine, he typically will replace it or refund your money.

America's numerous small vintners are committed to excellence. Their wine is produced by traditional wine-making techniques, with emphasis on the quality of the grapes, and the most successfully and scientifically proven processes.

As a broker, I specialize in American wines. Many wines from other countries are *among* the best in the world, but I feel American wines are simply *the* best in the world.

Chapter 5

Having Fun With Robert Parker: How to Distinguish Various Percentages of Truth in Wine Terminology Within 10 Seconds or Less

Have you ever read something or heard someone talk about a topic with words that don't quite fit your normal thought processes? When I first entered the wine business, I was much younger, more naive and paid little attention to those types of words. Now I do. This chapter is about confusing words some wine critics use to describe wine and why they use those words.

Hmmm! I wonder what Renaud means by "Various Percentages of Truth?" Maybe he means this chapter is going to be on how to recognize "bull."

THE PAGE TO READ

An artist I know once asked a wealthy customer how she was able to determine if a painting was great. The woman instantly replied, "By the price of the painting." An example that clearly demonstrates the prevalence of this attitude occurred in 1995 with the sale of a piece of the famous contemporary artist Tom Friedman's work at Christie's Auction House in New York City. It was titled *Starting An Old Dry Pen On a Piece of Paper* and consisted of a faint ink squiggle on a 12-inch by 18-inch sheet of white paper. Following fierce bidding, with a starting price of $14,000, the ink squiggle sold for $26,400.

In reality, there is no substance or talent to that type of artwork. This is a case of the artist, his broker and the gallery falsely correlating price with quality. These types of transactions, which are also common in the wine world, are simply exploitations of people with too much time and money at their disposal.

This also applies to the wine industry. There are no major, secret, hidden tastes in wines that only a handful of gifted palettes can identify. Every wine in the world is different. The price of a wine, the prestige of a vintner or a high score by a critic usually means a wine will be good to great. However, there are thousands of little-known vintners with unscored and "unbabbled" wines that are just as great. The following pages describe some of the hollow wine rhetoric often used to place wines in the upper echelons of finance.

The Hot Air Approach to Wine Language

Some in the wine industry are often more concerned about selling mystique and prestige than value and enjoyment. There are few other industries that depend almost totally on the opinion of a handful of self-proclaimed experts and critics to tell consumers if such a subjective product as wine is good, great or exquisite. As proof, when put to blind tests, experts seldom arrive at the same wine scores. In the end, there are only two people you can really depend on to identify a great or exquisite wine – you and your wine broker!

I find some consumers won't take a wine too seriously if it doesn't come with some type of a score. In spite of the highly individual nature of what constitutes a "great" or "exquisite" wine, the general wine drinking public is especially susceptible to wine scores that, in turn, are susceptible to various critics' tastes, which clearly vary, often to great degrees.

In her bestselling book, *The Wine Bible,* Karen MacNeil discusses the assessment of wine. MacNeil simply states: "One of the most insidious myths in American wine culture is that a wine is good if you like it. Liking a wine has nothing to do whether it is good. Liking a wine has to do with liking that wine, period." She goes on to say: "Wine requires two assessments: one subjective, the other objective. In this it is like literature. You may not like reading Shakespeare but agree that Shakespeare was a great writer nonetheless" and "Getting to the point where you are knowledgeable enough to have both a subjective and an objective opinion of wine is one of the most rewarding stages in developing wine expertise."

Although this is an excellent book, I disagree with that premise. Wine descriptions, like wine itself, are subjective and won't make a great wine better or worse. To me, if a wine is made with all the best ingredients, in the proper manner, and my wine customers think it is great, then it's great. A high score or feel-good description of a wine should never justify paying over $150 for the same quality of wine that can be purchased for $30 to $50. Wine priced in the $150 range is usually great according to someone's taste, but it often reaches that price level simply because it was given a high score and great descriptive narrative by some wine critic. Another factor may create an undeserved inflated price – wine may deliberately be made in small case amounts to create a forced scarcity and given a "this is so great it won't last long" attitude for the sake of commanding a higher, undeserved price.

I've never tasted a $100 to $200 bottle of wine that I couldn't equal or exceed in like quality and taste with a lower priced, but unscored or verbally unflattered, wine. An interesting exercise is to dissect some of the wine descriptions that accompany the scored wines – especially the Robert Parker-scored wines. The following descriptions tell more about Robert Parker's overexaggerated tastebuds than about the wines.

A Barrel of Dazzling Wine Words

The following are two of Robert Parker's typical hot air wine descriptions from his publication, the *Wine Advocate:*

2000 Chateauneuf du Pape Reserve des Celestins

It's no secret that I love the 2000 Chateauneuf du Pape Reserve des Celestins. While it may be sweet, jammy, and low in acidity, it is also voluptuous, sexy, super-ripe, and flattering. This big, juicy, fat 2000 reveals abundant quantities of kirsch liqueur intermixed with herbes de Provence, and that undefinable hint of prunes, fruitcake, sausage, and spice. It will be delicious when released, and will probably resemble the Reserve des Celestins 1985, which, by the way, is drinking great. I hope Bonneau will bottle the 2000 in 2003, since it does not appear to be a wine that will benefit from his extended elevage of 4-5 years. Anticipated maturity: 2003-2020. Rated 96-100, price wasn't determined yet.

2000 Chateauneuf du Pape Cuvee des Felix

The profound, opaque purple-colored 2000 Chateauneuf du Pape Cuvee des Felix elicited the following words: "Mama-Mia!" A fabulous offering, it provides a lesson in the flavors of Provence. It's like an open air Provincial marketplace with notes of dried herbs, saddle leather, fennel, licorice, black cherries, cassis, blackberries, and tapenade. With tremendous concentration and purity, as well as powerful, balanced, full-bodied flavors, this stunning effort represents the nectar of old vines planted in the sun-drenched appellation of Chateauneuf du Pape. Although more forward than the 1998, it is equally fragrant. Anticipated maturity: 2004-2020. Rated 96, price – $75.00.

The World of Cassis

Another example of an interesting Robert Parker wine description. He scored this wine a 96 and described it as follows:

> **"I was thrilled by the awesome quality of the 2001 La Joie, a blend of 71% Cabernet Sauvignon, 20% Merlot, and 9% Cabernet Franc. Aromas and flavors of roasted espresso, grilled herbs, scorched earth, blackberries, and cassis liqueur are accompanied by an unctuously-textured, full-bodied, expansive, dense, phenomenally concentrated, pure blockbuster. It should be at its finest between 2005-2020+. This is an out and out brilliant wine!"**

Don't be confused by the string of irrelevancies you often see written by some wine critics. When you see a description that sounds like nonsense, ask yourself why this description was said in a manner that sends you to your dictionary? The answer is simple: The authors of those types of descriptions simply want you to think they are highly sophisticated, intelligent, and just generally smarter than the average person, thus elevating their status as great wine connoisseurs and endearing themselves to other wine snobs. Basically, great wines are great wines, whether or not they are highly scored or liberally decorated with prose.

There are two words in this wine description I turned to my dictionary to learn – cassis and unctuously. Cassis wasn't in my *Webster's Ninth New Collegiate Dictionary*. However, I did find it in a French dictionary. Cassis is a "black currant fruit or black currant bush." Unctuous means 1. Smooth and greasy in texture or appearance. 2. Rich in organic matter and easily workable. 3. Full of unction, revealing or marked by a smug ingratiating, and false earnestness or spirituality."

If you can fool someone into believing you are an expert, you become, by illusion, an expert. This appears to be the case when it comes to wine-snob language and the numerous meaningless and uncomfortably inaccurate descriptions too often applied to wine. To me there's a sophisticated simplicity and integrity in using the limited yet applicable old-fashioned traditional descriptions from the pre-Parker era.

The bottom line should always be your personal choice. What tastes do you prefer in the wines you drink? Learn to know and describe those tastes to your wine broker or whomever you buy wine from.

The Parker Paradox

French
Wine

I find one of the most interesting facts in the wine world to be what I call the Parker Paradox. Robert Parker, an American, became the world's leading wine critic based on his professed claim that you didn't have to pay outrageous prices for great wine; all you had to do was follow his recommendations and you would discover affordable and excellent wines that were previously unknown. To go along with his boast, he also applied the 100-point grading system which he based on his somewhat personal peculiar taste for industrial objects.

The paradox: When Parker rates a wine above a 90, it automatically becomes one of the "best" wines in the world and reaches unaffordable, and typically unattainable, status. Worse yet, he has also become the premier champion of French wines, preferring and touting them far above the wines of his own country.

Traditional American
Wine Descriptions
You Can Count On

Aftertaste

Balanced

Brawny

Berry nose

Butterscotch

Buttery

Clean

Complex

Corked

Creamy

Crisp

Earthy

Firm

Flat

Flinty

Fresh

Fruit flavors (various descriptions)

Full bodied

Full mouth feel

Grapes (various varietals)

Grassy

Great balance

Hints of oak

Huge

Inky color

Lean

Long finish

Medium body

Moldy

Nice oak

Pruny

Rich

Ripe aromas

Silky

Smooth

Soft

Spicy

Strong tannin flavors

Sweet oak

Thick

Thin

Toasty oak

Upper mouth feel

Vanillin oak

Velvety

Vibrant

Vinegar

Young

Robert Parker Wine
Descriptions That Will Baffle You

Animal fur

Animal like character

Aromas of meat

Ashes

Asphalt

Balsamic vinegar in the

deep

Beet roots

Botrytis imbued apricots

Brambleberries

Buttered citrus

Camphor dried herbs

Candied white fruits

Caramelized minerals

Cassis

Charcoal

Chocolate covered figs

Chocolate mint ice cream

Clay stone

Compost

Crammed with stones

Creosote

Crunchy

Crushed minerals

Crushed rocks

Crushed stones

Extroverted

Exuberant

Fennel

Flamboyant

Forest floor

Garrigue

Graphite

Gravely

Grilled herbs

Heady

Incense

Iodine

Juniper smoked bacon

Kinky style

Kirsch

Lead pencil shavings

Liqueur rose pedal

Liquid stone character

Lovely panoply of flavors

Lychees

Melted asphalt

Melted road tar

Minerals

Monolithic character

Mulberries

Orestry

Papaya

Powdered stones

Root vegetables

Sandstone

Sassafras characteristics

Smoked game

Smoky hazelnuts

Tapenade

Tree bark

Underbrush

Verbena

Wet stones

White flowers

Wild cherries

Wood smoke

These descriptions were
taken from wine critic
Robert Parker's *Wine
Advocate* publications.

The Incredible Wine Word Machine

Question:
Do you know where pompous wine critics get their descriptive wine words?

Answer:
From the incredible auxiliary wine word machine.

Beware of Cult Wines

Cult wines emerged during the 1980s along with the widespread growth and upswing of the California wine industry. The term "cult wine" has no strict definition, although it typically applies to a wine that is made in limited quantities. Cult wines are usually costly, basically appealing to very wealthy people as trophy wines or status symbols. Once produced they are hyped to the point of creating a great demand, sending prices through the roof for the few bottles that actually make it to the open market.

To purchase a cult wine you have to get in on the ground floor with a spot on the winery's mailing list, or you got locked out and are forced to bid against scores of other cult followers when the wines come up at auction. The danger of purchasing a cult wine is there is no guarantee it will actually taste good or you will even like it. You are expected to buy without the opportunity of tasting and, if you don't buy, the next person on the list moves up. In my opinion, cult wines are designed more for selling and status than drinking. The hype and consequent mystique of a cult wine place it in a class of its own, regardless of its actual quality or whether it is truly unique. I would rather drink a proven great wine that I have tasted and know to be good than gamble on one coveted for its trophy status.

Vintners of cult wines often seek to persuade investors to invest in the future production of the wine. It is possible to make money through investing in certain top wines, but it is certainly not as easy as it is often suggested and the gains are often modest compared to the actual risks.

Chapter 6

Drinking Wine For Health Reasons

Wine and Longevity

The officially documented oldest person in the world was Jeanne Calment of France, who lived to the age of 122. Calment was born in 1875 and died in 1997. Among her claims for good health and longevity were that she rode a bicycle until she was 100 and consumed olive oil, port wine and chocolate. She enjoyed a piece of chocolate and a glass of port wine every day for most of her life.

The oldest officially documented man in the world was Sardinian Antonio Todde, who died in 2002 at the age of 111. When often asked the reason for his longevity, Todde's response was: "Just love your brother and drink a glass of red wine every day." Todde's basic diet was soup and pasta, with some pork or lamb each day, basically the Mediterranean diet. He also drank a glass and a half of red wine on a daily basis.

Enjoy a piece of chocolate and drink a glass of red wine every day.

Do you want to live a long, healthy life? Have you ever wondered what type of lifestyles those who reach the centenarian mark have lived, what they ate or drank, and what we can learn from successful examples? Many of the world's oldest living people, or those who have lived the longest, tend to have certain things in common besides good genes. Interestingly, among those things is the moderate consumption of wine as a beverage. Diet is another common factor. So, in addition to a discussion on the healthful benefits of moderate wine consumption, I have also included a little information on a healthy diet.

The French Paradox

In the early 1990s, a study was conducted at the University Bordeaux, with the objective of analyzing the effects of alcohol on our bodies. They set out to answer the question: How

Wine is good and good for you – in moderation. The volume of wine in this glass is _not_ considered moderate (but what she is actually drinking is sparkling cider).

can French people eat cream, pastries and cheese, yet suffer so few heart attacks? The conclusion was that if people with a typical French diet, which is rich in saturated fats, like animal fat, butter, pastries, etc., consumed moderate amounts of red wine, the risk of cardiovascular diseases was lowered.

On Sunday, November 17, 1991, the CBS show _60 Minutes_ aired a report they titled "French Paradox." This program featured interviews by Morley Safer with Boston University's Dr. Curtis Ellison, a cardiologist and professor at the School of Public Health; Dr. Monique Astier-Dumas, a nutritionist from Paris; and Dr. Serge Renaud, head of the French National Institute of Health and Medical Research. According to both Dr. Renaud and Dr. Ellison, the French custom of drinking wine with meals, at a moderate level, prevents coronary heart disease by as much as 50%. Since that time, more than 100 scientific reports have been published providing strong support in favor of the health benefits from moderate red wine consumption on a daily basis.

Why Drinking Wine Could Increase Your Life-Span

According to numerous studies, the properties in wine (especially red) responsible for the beneficial effects unique to wine are phenolic compounds, such as tannins and resveratrol that contain acidic disinfectant characteristics.

Tannins are an integral part of red wine and are important because of the antioxidants they contain. The red color and the sharp taste in wine both come from the skins of the grape. In addition to wine, tannins are also found in many other foods, such as nuts, cheeses and green tea. The bitter taste of tannins in plants prevent animals and insects from eating them, but are often found to be pleasurable to humans. The high concentration of tannins in red wine can sometimes cause mild to severe headaches.

Resveratrol (pronounced rez-VER-a-trawl) is a naturally occurring antioxidant compound found primarily in the skins of red grapes. Because of its chemical structure, resveratrol is also classified as a polyphenol. It has been identified in more than 70 species of plants including vines, roots, mulberries, blueberries, cherries, plum seeds, stalks, pine trees, peanuts and other plants. Red grapes, used to make wine, provide the most abundant source of this compound. The resveratrol content of wine is related to the length of time the grape skins are present during the fermentation process. The concentration is significantly higher in red wine than in white wine, because the skins are removed earlier during white-wine production. One fluid ounce of red wine averages 160 micrograms of resveratrol. Compare that to peanuts, which average 73 micrograms per ounce.

In the early 1990s, following the "French Paradox" study, researchers began to realize that the resveratrol content of wine was the secret ingredient behind the heart-healthy effects attributed to it. Since then, a diverse range of health problems that resveratrol appears to positively impact have been identified. They have also confirmed that the nutrients, minerals, vitamins and immune system boosters contained within red wine can promote substantial long-term health benefits. This is especially so for people at risk for heart disease as the result of a high fat, high cholesterol diet. (This research applied only to red wine.)

Although there are other touted health benefits from moderate alcohol consumption (especially red wine, because of the resveratrol), the two most notable pertain to the cardiovascular system and the prevention of cancer. Numerous laboratory studies throughout the nation have clearly demonstrated that resveratrol may reduce the incidence of coronary heart disease. In regards to how it affects the initiation, promotion and progression of cancer, it has been shown to act as an antioxidant by inhibiting free radical formation. (Recent studies have shown a correlation between alcohol consumption and an increased risk of breast cancer in women, but some studies suggest that red wine, because of the resveratrol, may actually *reduce* the risk. However, a warning against alcohol consumption that should never be compromised is for pregnant women. This is so important that a surgeon general warning is printed on alcohol bottle labels.)

The Mediterranean Diet

In addition to the basic life-style elements prevalent in the world's oldest living people, I have also recognized another common trait. Most of them have followed a diet consistent with what is generally known as the Mediterranean diet. It is not a narrowly defined program designed to fulfill a specific goal, such as weight loss, but is essentially a dietary life-style. Simply put, the diet is more plant than animal based. Extensive research has shown that people in the Mediterranean countries generally experience a lower rate of heart disease.

The Mediterranean is comprised of three continents and more than 15 countries, including Spain, France, Italy, Greece, Crete, Turkey, Syria, Lebanon, Israel, Egypt, Libya, Algeria and Morocco. All have influenced the so-called Mediterranean diet, but the Arabs are believed to have had the greatest impact, bringing nuts, saffron, rice, spinach and oranges into the region. The diets within these countries are not absolutely identical, but they all have the following similar and unique characteristics:

• Fruits, vegetables, bread and other cereals, potatoes, beans, nuts and seeds are mainstays.

• Olive oil, a principal source of fat in this diet, is high in healthy monounsaturated fat and is a good source of antioxidants. For more the 30 years, researches believed that olive oil was neutral with respect to its effects on cholesterol levels. However, current research has found olive oil and its high monounsaturated fat may actually increase HDL (good) cholesterol, but has little effect on LDL (bad) cholesterol.

• Dairy products, fish and poultry are consumed in low to moderate amounts, and only small amounts of red meat are eaten. Total red meat and poultry consumed is, on an average, about 15 ounces per week. Fish intake varies from country to country, but overall is slightly higher than meat or poultry.

• Eggs are consumed zero to four times a week.

• Throughout the Mediterranean, wine is consumed in moderation, usually with meals. For men, moderation is two five-ounce glasses per day; for women, one five-ounce glass per day.

Another significant factor is a more active lifestyle. The people of the Mediterranean incorporate physical activity into their daily lives. It is been well documented that exercise benefits physical, psychological and social well being and increases resistance to disease.

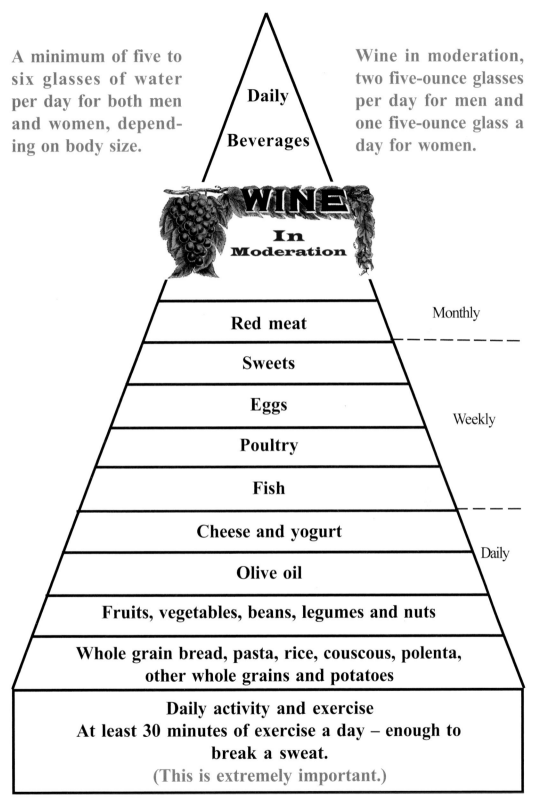

A minimum of five to six glasses of water per day for both men and women, depending on body size.

Wine in moderation, two five-ounce glasses per day for men and one five-ounce glass a day for women.

Daily

Beverages

WINE
In Moderation

Red meat — Monthly

Sweets

Eggs — Weekly

Poultry

Fish

Cheese and yogurt — Daily

Olive oil

Fruits, vegetables, beans, legumes and nuts

Whole grain bread, pasta, rice, couscous, polenta, other whole grains and potatoes

Daily activity and exercise
At least 30 minutes of exercise a day – enough to break a sweat.
(This is extremely important.)

The Mediterranean Health Pyramid.

Guide to a Long and Happy Life

Living a long time is good if lived in health and happiness. There are numerous elements of living that apply to this end – many physical and some spiritual. On the following page, I have outlined the best examples of these fundamentals in what I call "The Wine Rebel's Good Life & Longevity Pyramid." These principles are based on numerous studies of centenarians that, if followed, may be among the best advice ever taken.

Possibly the World's Most Healthy Diet

On an annual basis, various diet fads seem to come and go in quite dogmatic fashion. As each new fad hits the market, people hope for the miracles promised. Many of these new fads have proven to be ineffective and some even dangerous. I learned a long time ago that to find the best of anything you should take a look at both the successes and failures of your interests. Consequently, I recommend a Mediterranean type diet.

> The following, which appeared in the January 30, 2006 issue of *Time Magazine,* corroborates the wine for health concept:
>
> ### You Are What You Eat and Drink
> Danish scientists staked out grocery stores and found that people who buy wine instead of beer also buy healthier foods. Wine buyers purchased more olives, fruits, vegetables, poultry, low-fat milk and lean meat. Beer buyers rang up more cold cuts, chips, sausages, butter and sodas.

Please note that I recommend and write mostly about red wines. This is because red is the healthiest and I personally like it the best.

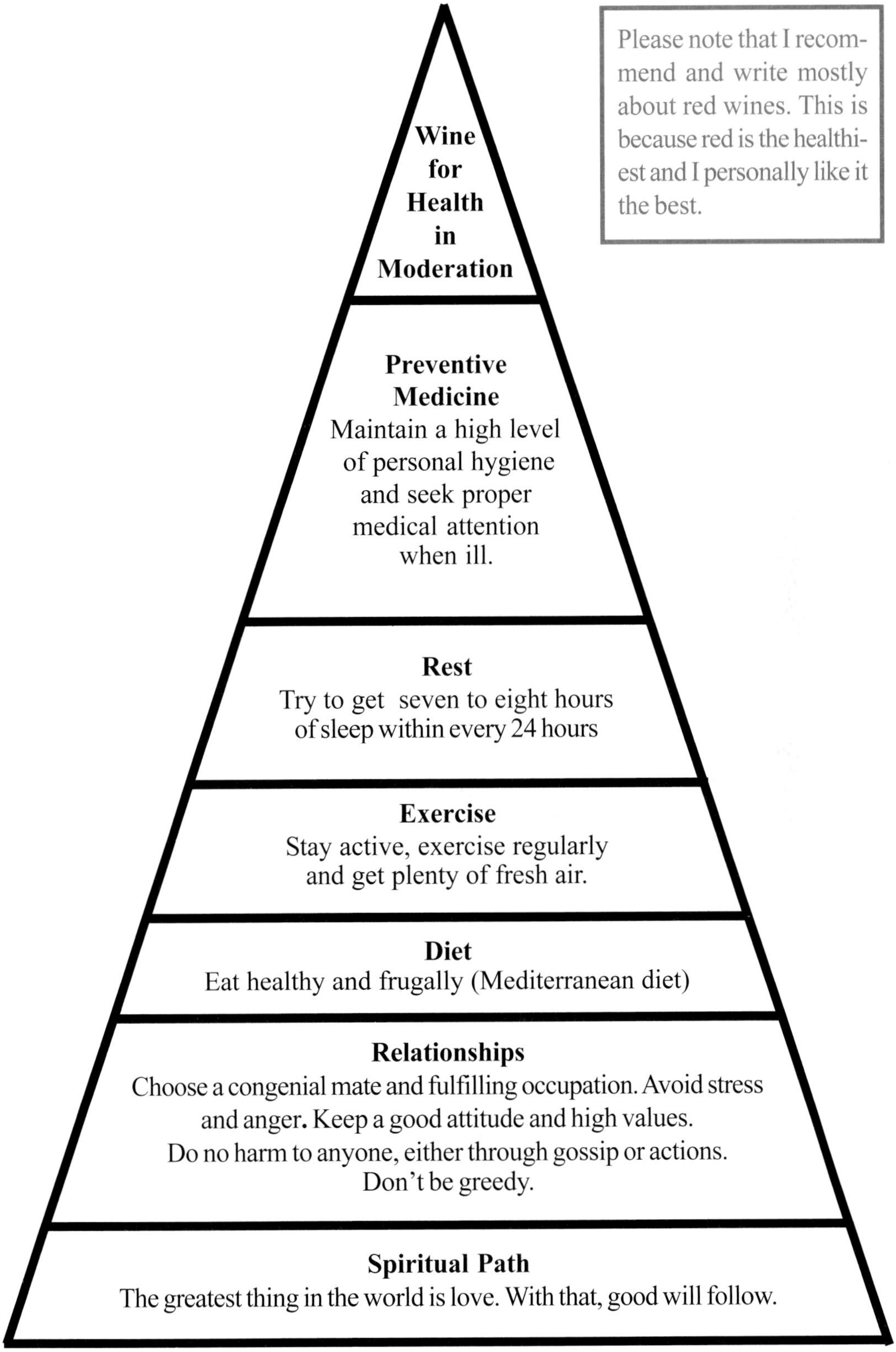
Wine for Health in Moderation
Preventive Medicine
Maintain a high level of personal hygiene and seek proper medical attention when ill.
Rest
Try to get seven to eight hours of sleep within every 24 hours
Exercise
Stay active, exercise regularly and get plenty of fresh air.
Diet
Eat healthy and frugally (Mediterranean diet)
Relationships
Choose a congenial mate and fulfilling occupation. Avoid stress and anger. Keep a good attitude and high values.
Do no harm to anyone, either through gossip or actions.
Don't be greedy.
Spiritual Path
The greatest thing in the world is love. With that, good will follow.

The Wine Rebel's Good Life & Longevity Pyramid

Man Before Etiquette Training

Man after Etiquette Training

An example of a man both before and after Renaud's etiquette training.

Chapter 7

Etiquette: The Key to Success and Happiness

Politeness and consideration are the easiest of all gifts to give others and also the most rewarding. Although *Webster's Dictionary* describes etiquette simply as the "conduct or procedure required by good breeding or prescribed authority to be observed in social or official life," the essence of etiquette may be considered the foremost characteristic that contributes to a sense of tranquility in our lives.

Throughout life's experiences, I often reflect on times when I've met someone and formed either an immediate bond, dislike or indifference toward them. There has always been a reason for each of my reactions, and was typically created by some type of interaction between us. If intense enough, the reaction may have left an indelible memory I am likely to carry throughout my lifetime.

At the end of the day, I usually review the contacts and interactions I have had, both good and bad. This often takes place in family discussions. Daily contacts generally fall into two categories: Those with people who have committed some act or gesture of kindness or consideration toward me or whom I have observed – those who sincerely try to make the world a better place to live and, in the process, are extraordinarily effective in all they do. The second category is with those whose rude actions or arrogant behavior have created an instant negative reaction or dislike for that person.

I find it helpful to mentally critique the actions of the people with whom I have contact as a way to improve my own behavior. By introspecting about my wins and losses in life, I can usually see my mistakes. The wins in my life have clearly resulted from good etiquette in some form. The losses have come, deservedly so, from bad manners or inconsiderate conduct. The key to success sounds pretty simple, doesn't it? Practice good etiquette and the world will be yours, or at the least you will be doing your part to make life more pleasant for those around you, and also feel good about yourself.

No book about wine would be complete without talking about etiquette. Wine, to me, is about life, harmony, comfort and all that generates a sense of goodwill towards others. What better way is there to cultivate this than by practicing good manners and simple etiquette? Basic everyday etiquette is at the root of proper wine etiquette, and has a great deal to do with using good old common sense Because I feel my understanding of etiquette has made me a better person, and is important to most people, I am going to touch on some of the key elements of *basic* etiquette before discussing *wine* etiquette. The most successful, loved and respected people I know, or know about, possess the following traits. Although there are many ways to show kindness and consideration, if these nine most valuable etiquette guidelines are applied whenever possible, I believe your presence will brighten the lives of family, friends and colleagues alike.

Basic Etiquette

1. Show respect and consideration, behave toward others as you would like them to behave towards you: Just starting out in my career in my early twenties, I got a job in sales. I worked hard and was determined to excel at this job. Quickly becoming one of the top salesmen in the company, I was being considered for my own distributorship. Around this time, the company held its annual party. The company manager was seated at the center of a large table. Dave, another leading salesman whom I knew well and considered a friend, was seated next to him. During the course of the evening, Dave got up to use the restroom, and I moved to his chair. When Dave returned, he sat in the chair I had just vacated, and I spent the remainder of the evening conversing with our boss. The following day, arriving at the office to receive my assignment, the manager took me aside and gently chided me for my inconsideration. This man was truly a gentleman in his manner of confrontation and, although I couldn't have felt much lower, he gave me one of the most important lessons pertaining to social graces I have ever received. Reflecting back, I realized I hadn't really seized an opportunity to better myself, but had been insensitive towards my colleague and friend. My boss had tolerated it to avoid embarrassing me, yet was gracious enough to give me valued advice.

2. Be polite and complimentary: Reflect for a moment on people you know who display these qualities. You immediately feel comfortable around them, don't you? This is one of the easiest ways to bring goodwill your way. Even spending one day at your local library reading a book on etiquette, and then applying the lessons learned, will enhance your life and relationships. People love to receive compliments. However, what you compliment is significant. I've always felt there's a big difference between what a person acquires versus what they achieve. A compliment for an achievement is far more deserved, and often more appreciated.

3. Be a good listener: A good rule of thumb, in my opinion, is when someone wants to tell you something, let them exhaust what they have to say without interrupting them. Respond only when asked, or where appropriate, during the conversation. If someone really wants to know about you or your views, they'll ask. If not, simply be a good listener. It's the polite thing to do, and you'll leave a great impression with that person as someone she or he enjoys talking to.

4. Cleanliness: This one should be obvious.

5. Humility: Think of those people you know who are "full of themselves" to the point of being boastful. Most of us find that behavior repulsive. Do you want to be like them?

6. Admit fault and apologize when necessary: This is a quality that truly identifies the character of a person. It shows humility and a strength of character to admit fault and apologize. We all know people who will never admit to making mistakes, or apologize for wrongs they've committed. Do you trust or admire that type of person?

7. Be sincere and appreciative: This must come from the heart and can be expressed with a simple "thank you," cards, letters or, where appropriate, hugs.

8. Don't be a loudmouth, dominating conversations, cursing or using vulgar language: To realize the impact of this conduct, just look at those people who behave in this manner and assess your feelings toward them.

9. Never laugh at, or take delight in, another's mistakes or misfortune: This is simply mean spirited. We all make mistakes, and we will all suffer misfortune in our lives at some point or another.

Wine Tasting Protocol in Restaurants

There are major differences between wine, beer and spirits. Besides being among nature's best health drinks when consumed in moderation, wine has typically been the predominant beverage chosen for special occasions. As such, it is often attended by some type of sophisticated presentation or simple ritual of honor. Some understanding of the basic rules of wine etiquette will serve you throughout your lifetime. This knowledge will also enhance the enjoyment and full appreciation of your wine experiences.

One of the first essentials for ordering wine in a restaurant is to determine what varietal of  wine you prefer. You should know this beforehand. The term wine varietal refers to the grape from which the wine is made, such as Cabernet Sauvignon, Merlot, Pinot Noir or Syrah. By law, to label the wine as such, it must contain at least 75% of that grape varietal. Varietals of wine each have their own distinctive grape flavors and characteristics, which will vary from winery to winery and from region to region. The aromas and flavors of a wine will depend on the location of the vineyards, how they are managed, and most importantly, the vintner's recipe for making this wine.

As proof of its prestige in the world of fine dining, wine glasses are normally included in the basic table setting of America's best restaurants in anticipation of arriving guests. The wine order will typically signal the beginning of a special evening of dining out. A ritual of selection, presentation, testing and approval will follow.

The host, or person who has invited the guests, is expected to pay for, and to select, the wine for the meal. However, friends getting together casually often agree ahead of time to "go Dutch" or split the tab. The honor of selection may be offered to a guest as a sign of respect for their knowledge and taste in wine. Advice can also be sought from other guests or the wine steward. If you ask advice from a wine steward, or *sommelier*, it is best to give as specific parameters as possible – price range, type or varietal of wine, and the purpose for which it is intended. If you do ask the wine server for a suggestion, you may also want to ask if they have personally tasted the wine they just recommended.

What to look for in a wine: When you taste a wine, you are doing so to determine if you like it. How it tastes to you is what matters the most. Some wine aficionados have a language and ritual of their own for tasting, which can be intimidating to the novice. It is often confusing verbiage and often seen as an attempt to impress. The wine tasting ritual is typically used when dining in fine restaurants. However, in my opinion, it can easily turn into an overblown ritual of egotistical showmanship. Basically, this is a simple ritual that can add a touch of class to your dining experience. Remember, when all is said and done, the people who serve you or own the restaurant want your money and, in fact, will be taking some of it. So, unless you are completely rowdy, rude or obnoxious in some manner, they will want you to come back with more of your money. Consequently, sniffing the cork or other ill-informed wine etiquette will not get you thrown out of the restaurant, but you may later be scoffed at behind your back.

The presentation and examination of wine in a restaurant is one of the most overstated and misunderstood rituals in the wine culture. It involves six simple procedures that can very easily be accomplished in a short period of time in a quiet and dignified manner. These procedures should be carried out by the person who orders the wine. I recommend letting the sample sit in the glass for a few minutes before tasting it. I don't feel it is at all inappropriate to ask the server for a few minutes to let the wine open up.

Menu,

How to amaze your friends and order wine in a classy restaurant

Six Simple Procedures

1. Presenting of wine by the waiter or wine steward: The wine you've ordered is presented to you. While your presenter holds it, you are expected to look at the label and verify it's what you ordered. This should take four to five seconds. Unless you are presented with something you didn't order, your response should be "thank you!" and the server will proceed.

Presentation of wine by the wine server.

2. Uncorking the bottle: Next, your wine server will cut and remove all or part of the foil concealing the cork, remove the cork and lay it in front of you. Once this is done, do not sniff the cork. You may do two things with the cork – ignore it or make a quick examination to verify the name of the winery, year the wine was bottled or other imprinted information. There are some potential cork problems to look for, but they are typically rare and can be spotted quickly. For example, only the bottom portion of the cork should be stained. If wine has seeped all the way to the top of the cork, the wine got hot at

Uncorking the wine.

A good example of an unsophisticated wine patron. Mark, the man in lower picture, is doing a number of things wrong. He is sniffing the cork, definitely frowned on in classy wine circles. As a result, notice the look of embarrassment on his table companion's face. In addition, his tie is too short and he has a "nerd pac" in his shirt pocket. Other than that, he looks like a nice guy who just needs some helpful etiquette guidance.

some point and may be bad. If a bottle of wine was not laid on its side during long periods of storage, the cork often becomes dry. This may have allowed air into the wine, causing it to spoil. If you do wish to examine the cork, a four to five second examination is enough, unless you find something drastically wrong with it. Remember, don't make a big deal about the cork.

3. Pouring the wine for you to examine: Next, your wine server will pour a small amount of wine in your glass. You are expected to examine it. This is easy and should take no longer that five to six seconds. However, again I recommend letting the sample sit in the glass for a few minutes to allow the wine to open up.

Pouring the wine.

4. Examining the wine you have just been presented: Do you know what you are really looking for here? Unless your wine is some type of obnoxious color or contains a large amount of sediment, bits of cork, large unidentified floating matter or anything gross-looking in it, it's no big deal and should not be dwelled upon.

Wine is typically consumed from a clear glass (my favorite is a rocks glass) in order to see the color of the wine. The color of red wine is typically in varying shades of maroon, purple, ruby, garnet, red or even brownish. White wine should be clear, straw-like, golden,

To appreciate the color, serve red wine in clear glasses.

light green, pale yellow or slightly brown or shades in between these colors. When looking at wine, what can you possibly say about the color of a wine that would appear to put you in the know? Others at your table are probably watching you look at the wine and hoping you will hurry up so they can start enjoying it. No comment about the color is necessary.

Another observation often made in this examination process is about the wine's "legs." Legs, or tears as the French refer to them, are the streaks of wine forming on the side of the wine glass. During wine presentations, you often see someone swirl a glass of wine, raise it towards the light and watch for the legs to appear. This is a mythical indicator of wine quality. The legs were once thought to be associated with a wine's quality (the more legs, the higher the quality). In reality, the legs you see coming down the insides of your glass are created by the wine's surface tension and its alcohol content. They have no relationship to the quality of the wine, so don't bother commenting on the legs.

5. Smell the wine: Before tasting the wine, you should smell it. Your tongue can sense only four tastes: sweet, sour, salt, and bitter, but your nose can differentiate thousands of distinct aromas. Swirl the wine in the glass. This is done by holding the base of the glass on a flat surface and making a tight counterclockwise circle. Swirling has two purposes. It moves the wine to coat the side of the glass and allows more of it to be exposed to air,

Here's Louie the Wine Examiner in a relaxed casual setting. Notice how he is examining and smelling the contents of his glass of wine. He appears to be carefully looking for obnoxious color, large amounts of sediment, bits of cork, large unidentified floating matter or anything gross looking. This often times proves to be a helpful procedure, and it definitely leaves an impression on those around him.

which releases the aromas, and it allows the sulfurs to evaporate more quickly. Take a whiff of your freshly poured glass of wine, then swirl it, stick your nose into the glass, and take another sniff. The motion gives you a burst of aroma. White wines smell of citrus or tropical fruits, while reds vary from berries to earth to wood tones. If spoiled, it will smell like vinegar, rotten eggs or dirty socks. The wine smelling process should not last over four to five seconds, unless it really smells bad, in which case you would decline it and, in harmony with your wine server, select a new bottle.

Here's Louie again – in a different setting. This time he's secluded himself in a quiet location for the tasting phase of the wine examination process. Notice the intense concentration on his face. It is obvious Louie takes this process seriously.

6. Tasting the wine: This is easy, unless the wine is obviously bad. If there is any problem with the wine, in that it is spoiled or corked (meaning it has been tainted by defective cork, giving it a musty taste – see page 214), this is the time to decide if the wine will be served. Wine can be refused for legitimate cause, but not because a person regrets the choice. Upon approval, which is always to be expected unless the wine is truly defective, give your wine server a nod or a polite comment of approval. Your wine server will then serve the wine to all at your table. Once a wine has been accepted, it is generally served in a clockwise manner, with ladies first. The first glass may be offered to the guest of honor. The host will have his glass filled last. Wine will always taste better if allowed to breathe for a few minutes.

Corkage

No restaurant is able to carry every wine no matter how impressive their wine cellar. In order to provide the greatest service and enjoyment to their guests, many restaurants offer corkage, the practice of allowing guests to bring in a bottle or bottles of wine to accompany their meal. There is generally a charge for corkage, which can vary. The purpose is to allow guests to bring in a special or rare wine they wish to share. It is not considered appropriate to bring in a wine that is on the wine list offered by the establishment. If you desire to bring in a bottle, you should call ahead to determine if this is an accepted policy, what the corkage fee is, and if there are any doubts whether or not it is a wine offered by the restaurant. This will prevent any embarrassing moments. The wine is generally served by the wine steward/sommelier in a manner similar to that of a bottle ordered from the restaurant.

Here's Mark again. This time he brought his own wine to a restaurant, not just one bottle but four, with one even stuffed in his pants pocket. This guy might have trouble fitting in socially with the more sophisticated groups in his area. On the bright side, he's adjusted his tie length to the proper length and removed his nerd pac.

Corkage fees range in price from nothing to $50. I have a standard rule of thumb. If the corkage fee is over $20, I am left with the impression that I am being discouraged from bringing my own wine and will find another more welcoming restaurant. Or, if you are going to pay someone $20 to remove a cork from a bottle of wine brought to the restaurant, why not consider applying that amount to a bottle purchased from the restaurant? This also gives you a chance to experiment with different wines.

My advice to people who bring their own wine to a restaurant: This should be done only if the restaurant does not stock a special wine you want to share with your guests. Dining out should always be a pleasant experience for all involved.

My advice to owners and managers of restaurants is to always be mindful that you are in the hospitality business. Design your policies to be welcoming to your clientele. Remember, the people who bring their own wine to your place of business will have friends and their friends will have friends. A little bad word goes a long way.

Never upset the cooks or waiters. Who knows what they will put in your food?

In 1919, Louis Davenport, the founder of Spokane's historic Davenport Hotel wrote a five-page article for a business journal published in Muskegon, Michigan, called *System*. A short excerpt from that article describes one of the keys to his success:

> You can plan to make your mechanical equipment practically foolproof, but it is very much harder to train employees always to express the house policy. Yet in the last analysis it is through employees that the house policy must be principally expressed. A surly look or discourteous word is more than enough to banish in a second all memory a guest may have of a comfortable bed or an exceptional meal.

Wine Steward or Sommelier?

The word *sommelier* is the French term for a specialist wine waiter or wine steward in a restaurant, and is one of the most mispronounced wine terms. Amusingly, many American wine stewards also mispronounce their own title when they refer to themselves as *sommeliers*. Most American wine stewards pronounce the word *sommelier* (som.mol.yeah, or som-mol-e-yeah). French *sommeliers* typically pronounce it (soom-merl-e-a, or sawm-uhl-yeah). The word is derived from the word *sommier,* which comes from the Latin *sagmarium*, meaning "the man responsible for the cargo, or the burden of a pack train." The word *sommier*, by extension, soon came to mean the animal's cargo. The *sommier* later evolved more specifically to refer to the pack train's cargo as "chests with goods locked inside." The man in charge of these chests eventually began to be known as the *sommelier* or the official in charge of transporting (by packhorse) all the belongings that traveled with princes and aristocrats.

Since the Middle Ages, the term *sommelier* was used in France to denote the principal wine taster of a religious order or royal household, and it has been used by the French ever since.

Sometimes there's a fine line between two names for the same thing. In these photos the wine steward for the famous Davenport Hotel in Spokane, Washington, demonstrates the difference between a sommelier on the left and a wine steward on the right.

The American Wine Steward

For the purposes of this manual, I will refer to the French counterpart as a *sommelier* and the American as wine steward. Both are typically restaurant employees who buy and maintain the wines sold in the restaurant, and usually have extensive knowledge concerning wines. The wine steward typically may have many other responsibilities, which vary depending on the size and sophistication of the restaurant.

In many elegant restaurants, the wine steward characteristically serves as an ambassador for the restaurant, taking on more of a marketing and public relations role. His attire will usually make him stand out from the other wait staff members.

In restaurants without a *sommelier*/wine steward, the server will handle both the food and wine selections and ordering. Many Americans have never heard of the word *sommelier*, which can be confusing when heard for the first time. There's the story of the restaurant patron who asked his waiter if he could order some wine. The waiter asked him if he would like the *sommelier*, to which the customer replied, "Yes, please, that's a great idea." When the *sommelier* came to the table, he asked the customer if he would like to see the wine list. The customer replied, "No, thank you, I just ordered a bottle of *sommelier*." Unless I am in France, I prefer to use the term "wine steward."

The sequential reactions of an American wine steward before, during and after tasting a 98-point scored wine that contains hints of compost and melted road tar.

Serving Wine at Home

In preparing to entertain guests in your home, there are many items to consider: occasion, decorations, food and beverage. If wine is the beverage of choice, there are a few preparations which will enhance its presentation and enjoyment. After the wines have been selected, know the proper temperature at which each wine is at its optimum.

Appropriate temperatures for storing wine: 56 to 60 degrees is sufficient for all wines.

Uncorking wines: Red wines should be uncorked and placed in a decanter or glass approximately one-half hour before they are to be served. This allows the sulfur to escape. White wines should be opened just a few minutes prior to serving.

Decanting wine: Decades ago, it was common for wines to contain a considerable degree of solid matter. The decanting process involved pouring wine from a bottle that had remained still for a long enough time to allow any sediment to fall to the bottom of the container. The contents would then be carefully poured into another clean container. With the exception of wines 10 years or older, most wines on the shelves today have no real need for decanting for clarification purposes, as the wine making process ensures the wine is thoroughly clarified before it is bottled. There are a number of processes employed to remove insoluble substances that can cause cloudiness, such as filtering and fining. (For a discussion about clarifying processes, see pages 207-208).

Serving: When serving wine, ladies should be served first. The bottle is held to allow the label to be read. The bottle should never touch the lip of the glass. A napkin should be carried to catch or prevent drips. When pouring, fill the glass halfway or to the widest area of the glass. This leaves sufficient room to swirl the wine allowing for the full presentation of its bouquet. Once red wine is poured into the glass, it should sit for 10 to 15 minutes.

Leftover wine: By pumping the air out of open bottles with a vacuum pump, the remaining wine will stay fresh for an average of 5-7 days.

American Dining Etiquette

Throughout the average person's lifetime there will be occasions that call for certain basic social skills. These occasions may include an important business-related dinner, a romantic date at an expensive restaurant, a first dinner at the home of a new romantic interest, or simply a dinner with respected friends.

A sophisticated knowledge of table etiquette is not difficult to learn and will remain with you your entire life. Once learned, this basic knowledge becomes an important part of your total being. Good manners are the mark of a person. They not only place you at a higher level of social acceptance, they show you have respect for others.

A dinner setting for two at Spokane's historic Davenport Hotel. In 2006, the Davenport Hotel was named among the top ten hotels in the nation for customer satisfaction and was ranked fifth among AAA-rated four-star hotels. Although there is no absolute standard of correctness, this photo depicts a core formal dinner place setting. It includes: 1. cloth napkin, 2. dinner fork, 3. butter knife, 4. charger plate (restaurant customs vary, but if used, it is generally removed prior to placement of the main entree or with the main entree plate), 5. dinner knife (serrated edge pointing towards the plate), 6. water glass, and 7. various wine glasses. As you order other items, they will come with the appropriate silverware, such as appetizer, coffee or dessert.

Holding the silverware

Both spoon and fork are typically held horizontally by balancing them between the first knuckle of the middle finger and the tip of the index finger while the thumb steadies the handle. The knife should be held with the tip of the index finger pressing out over the top of the blade to guide as you cut.

Cutting meat

When foods, such as meat, require the use of both a knife and fork to obtain a bite of manageable size, the fork should be switched to the left hand. The tines of the fork are pointed downward to hold the meat in place while the right hand operates the knife. After a bite-sized piece has been cut, the diner sets the knife down on the plate and transfers the fork to the right hand. Only cut and consume one bite at a time.

What to do with used utensils

The basic rules regarding the placement of used flatware is never to lay them on the table or tablecloth. Your knife should be placed along the edge of your plate when not in use.

The start of the meal

When everyone is seated, remove the napkin from your place setting, unfold it, and put it across your lap. At some very formal restaurants, the waiter may do this for the diners, but it is also perfectly appropriate to place your own napkin in your lap. If your napkin falls on the floor during a formal event, don't pick it up; ask your server for a new one. When you leave the table at the end of the meal, place your napkin loosely next to your plate. It should not be crumpled, twisted, or folded.

It is typically customary to wait to take a bite until everyone at the table has received a serving and your host has begun eating. Sometimes your host may urge guests to eat immediately upon receiving the food. This is especially true at larger events, where waiting for everyone would allow it to get cold. If so, wait until one or two of the other guests are also ready to begin. You should not be the only person at the table who is eating.

Posture

Sit up straight, with your arms held near your body. While eating, you should neither lean on the back of the chair nor bend forward to place the elbows on the table (and, in most circles, it is considered quite improper to put your feet on the table). Also, never tilt back on your chair. During your meal, your left (or non-dominant) hand should remain in your lap unless needed for cutting. If your food requires using both hands, such as with a sandwich, it is appropriate to use both hands.

Passing the salt or pepper

The proper response to this request is to pick up both the salt and the pepper and to place them on the table within reach of the person next to you, who will do the same, and so on, until they reach the person who asked for them.

Eating soup

Dip the spoon into the soup and move it away from the body until it is about two-thirds full, then sip the liquid (without slurping) from the side of the spoon (without inserting the whole bowl of the spoon into the mouth). It's okay to tilt the bowl slightly, again away from the body, to get the last spoonful or two of soup.

When in doubt, don't drink it!

Sometimes it's hard to recognize a finger bowl as these are typically used in the classiest of dining establishments. If you ever receive one it will happen either before or after the dessert course. They typically look like small bowels containing water. Once you recognize that you have a finger bowl, all you need to know is that you should dip your fingertips in the water, dry them off with your napkin, and set the bowl to the side of your plate.

Does this even need to be said?

No doubt your mother coached you on this one: Never talk with your mouth full. Also eat slowly and chew your food thoroughly. **(According to numerous statistics, thousands of people die annually from choking to death on food.)**

Tipping

Server: 15% of bill (excluding tax) for adequate service; 20% for very good service; no less than 10% for poor service.
Bartender: 15% to 20% of the tab, with a minimum of 50 cents per soft drink, $1 per alcoholic drink.
Sommelier or wine steward: 15% of cost of the bottle.
Parking valet or garage attendant: $2 to bring your car to you.
Taxi driver: Varies depending on locality. Assume 15% will be enough; an extra $1 to $2 for help with bags.
Coatroom attendant: $1 per coat.
Washroom attendant: 50 cents to $1.
Musician in lounge: $1-5.

Quality of Service

If the service is poor, talk to the manager. Restaurant owners, through their managers, want to know how their customers are being treated, as their business depends on it. Managers can't correct situations they don't know about.

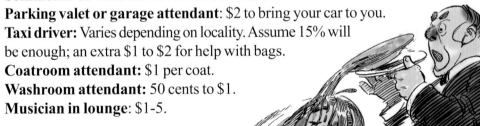

Wine Glasses

There are hundreds of various wine glasses to choose from. However, there are two basics. Typical wine glasses have stems and are clear glass to enable the wine to be seen. The larger glasses are customarily used for red wine and the smaller for white wine. Some people, including myself, prefer to use rocks glasses (left photo at bottom), or even paper cups, depending on the situation and location. The wider the mouth of a glass, the more the wine is able to breathe.

One consideration I learned early in life was the importance of flowers. Flowers are probably the most inexpensive way to gain someone's attention and appreciation. Think of the emotional responses you have received from someone to whom you have given flowers or your response when given flowers. Remember the expression your often hear: "Say it with flowers." Well! There really is a language of flowers and it's a great way to communicate.

Language of Flowers

There is a certain aura of romance attached to the combination of wine and flowers. Both are often used in settings to convey the message of a heartfelt emotion. Think back at your occasions that included wine, candlelight, flowers, and how your cares seemed to melt away.

In an era gone by, flowers were believed to have magical powers and, for centuries, were given a place of honor, with a meaning assigned to each flower. The following partial list of definitions are from the *Victorian Era Language of Flowers Dictionary,* which are still in use by those who wish to receive high courting or marriage evaluations:

Carnation, white – sweet and lovely, pure and deep love
Carnation, pink – I'll never forget you
Carnation, red – my heart aches for you; admiration
Cedar leaf – I live for you
Clover, four-leafed – be mine
Daffodil – unrequited love
Daisy, garden – innocence, loyal love, purity
Geranium, rose – I prefer you
Ivy – friendship, marriage
Lilac – first emotions of love
Lily, white – majesty, purity
Lily of the Valley – return of happiness
Magnolia – love of nature
Marigold – sacred affection
Mistletoe – I surmount everything
Morning glory – affection
Olive – peace
Pansy, purple – you occupy my thoughts
Rosebud – confession of love
Rose, red – I love you
Rose, white – silence, purity
Rose, wild single – simplicity
Tulip, red – declaration of love
Violet, blue – faithfulness
Violet, white – purity, modesty

Quam bene vivas refert, non quam diu.

(The important thing isn't how long you live but how well you live.)

Chapter 8

Memorable Wine-Drinking Destinations
From High to Low Places – A Glimpse of the West

I sell wine throughout the United States, a country that is blessed with some of the greatest wine-drinking destinations in the world. In my opinion, California wine country, where I grew up and established my career, and the Inland Northwest, where I now reside and transact my business, offer some of the choicest places to enjoy a glass of great American wine. This chapter is intended to showcase some of my favorite destination spots in these two regions. As the title suggests, although difficult to find, there are "low" wine-drinking destinations. Keep reading, as you will no doubt be surprised by the lowest of them all!

The Monroe Street Bridge, one of Spokane's most recognizable and historic landmarks, was touted as the longest concrete-arch bridge structure in the world at the time of its construction in 1911. On September 17, 2005, following a two-year, $18-million restoration, Spokane's famous bridge was reopened. This, and the following photos, were taken on the occasion of the grand-reopening celebration.

Celebrants at the grand reopening of the Monroe Street Bridge. The photo at the top right shows the view of the Spokane River below the bridge.

Site of the 1974 World's Fair,
held in Spokane, Washington.

Looking east at a section of the beautiful Spokane falls in the heart of downtown Spokane, the largest city in the Inland Northwest. The Spokane River runs west from Coeur d'Alene, Idaho, through the city of Spokane, and on to the Columbia River. During the 1974 World's Fair, the structure visible beyond the bridge supported the largest tent in the world.

Following Spokane's hosting of the 1974 World's Fair, the site became Riverfront Park. The building closest to the river houses the historic Looff Carrousel, built in 1909, which is a main attraction in the park.

A Book of Verses underneath the Bough,
A Jug of Wine, a Loaf of Bread – and Thou
Beside me, singing in the Wilderness –
Oh, Wilderness were Paradise enow!
From *The Rubaiyat of Omar Khayyam*, 1100 AD.

I often associate good times with dining out and fine wine. Over the years, I have gained an interesting insight into the fine dining business. You can typically judge the quality of the restaurant by the wines they serve. A great restaurant is often frequented by those who know and appreciate good wines. Consequently, the owners and management of those better dining establishments will employ waiters, or wine servers, who have an expertise in wine, especially those with the ability to recognize great tasting wines. Further, professional wine experts will never purchase wine they have not tasted and cannot personally recommend. This just makes good sense, as most fine restaurants typically strive for a markup of about three to four times their cost. The vast majority of wines sold in fine restaurants are in the $35 to $50 range. One bottle of wine fills four wine glasses. That's $12.50 per glass for a $50 bottle or $8.50 for a $35 bottle. For that price, you should be able to expect your wine servers to have a taste-knowledge of the wines the restaurant has to offer, as you are paying for their expertise.

The following pages feature some fine dining establishments in Spokane and Coeur d'Alene, all of which feature excellent choices of domestic wines.

The Wine Rebel and a view of downtown Spokane from the South Hill.

The Davenport Hotel in Spokane, Washington, is Among the Top 10 Hotels in America

This restaurant and hotel, Spokane's most popular landmark, has been attracting some of the world's most famous people since the 1890s. Following a complete restoration by owners Walt and Karen Worthy, it reopened in 2002 (inset), and continues to be one of the Inland Northwest's great destination spots. In 2006, it ranked fifth among AAA-rated four-star hotels in the nation by Expedia.com and among the top 10 hotels in the United States for customer satisfaction.

The author and his wife enjoying a glass of wine and a view of downtown Spokane from the balcony of the Davenport Hotel's presidential suite.

Tom McArthur (left), Director of Communications for the Davenport Hotel. On the right, the author and his wife, Shawna, examine some of the many excellent American wines the Davenport includes on its wine list.

A Davenport Hotel guest seated next to the bronze sculpture of the hotel's founder, Louis M. Davenport, whose establishment put Spokane on the map in the 1890s.

A romantic evening in the Marie Antoinette Room. This was the hotel's grand ballroom when constructed in 1914. The dance floor was built on springs to gently move with the dancers. When the hotel was restored in 2000-2002, a larger ballroom was constructed. This room is used for many banquets and special events.

Toasting with wine in the Isabella Room of the Davenport Hotel.

At the baby grand piano in the Presidential Suite of the Davenport Hotel. During the restoration, the main public rooms of the hotel were returned to their original, historic beauty. The guest room floors were gutted and replaced with entirely new construction, which enabled the hotel to create beautifully appointed, palatial guest rooms with all the modern conveniences and state-of-the-art safety standards.

The beautifully restored lobby of Spokane's exquisite Davenport Hotel. The hotel offers its guests a variety of dining options. Guests can enjoy an elegant meal in the Palm Court Restaurant, or enjoy more casual dining in the lobby or the Peacock Lounge, but still have the benefit of ordering from the same menu.

Tasting wine in the Isabella Room of the Davenport Hotel. This elegant room, which originally served as the hotel's formal dining room, is simply breathtaking. Today it is a popular location for weddings and other formal events.

Clinkerdagger's Restaurant
in Spokane's Old Flour Mill on the Spokane River

The old C&C Flour Mill, a Spokane landmark, was built in 1895. It now houses Clinkerdagger's Restaurant (shown below during the Christmas season) and other restaurants, shops, retail businesses and offices.

Clinkerdagger's Old English decor and view of the Spokane River, coupled with its excellent cuisine and service, make it a popular dining spot. It has a reputation for fresh seafood, rock salt roasted prime rib, and unsurpassed burnt cream dessert, and has received numerous awards, including "Best of Spokane."

Luna, located on Spokane's South Hill

"The most promising restaurant to ever open in Spokane." The Spokesman-Review

Luna was created by a married couple, William and Marcia Bond (below left), who left their respective professions to join forces in opening a lively, joyful Spokane South Hill neighborhood restaurant. It took a year to find the right location, a former produce market at Fifty-Seventh Avenue and South Perry Street, and a total renovation ensued. The eclectic menu features Northwest cuisine and includes wild salmon, halibut, roasted chicken, grilled steaks, marinated Small Planet tofu and pizza-plus from an applewood-fired stone oven. Since the beginning, the owners and entire staff have been deeply committed to offering fresh, local, healthy and incredibly tasty food, exquisite ambiance and joyful service. This commitment has been realized every day since it opened on November 26, 1993.

The Spokesman-Review has named Luna the number one restaurant in Spokane in four separate years. Among others, *Northwest Best Places* (who named them number one in Spokane in 2006), *Northwest Travel Guide,* and *Wine Spectator* have honored them with recognition and awards. The restaurant's growing popularity necessitated the need for a recent expansion. It now has 2,400 square feet of dining space, including the main dining room, the Garden Room for private dining, a full service bar, and the Rose Terrace and Sunset Courtyard for outdoor dining.

Luna takes pride in its wine list and in offering affordable wines to be enjoyed while dining. They stock 700 various labels from the Northwest, California and at least a dozen foreign countries. They also have 100 wines under $25, and several hundred cases aging in a deep cellar.

Anthony's Homeport at Spokane Falls,
overlooking the Spokane River

Anthony's Homeport Restaurant on the Spokane River is one of 23 throughout Washington State. Anthony's is known for fresh seafood (they own their own seafood company), waterfront views and warm, friendly service. Most importantly, for the theme of this manual, they feature Northwest wines.

Enjoying lunch at Anthony's Restaurant.

Fresh Dungeness crab from the Pacific Northwest is simply the best!

Coeur d'Alene, Idaho, and the Surrounding Region, the Inland Northwest's Premier Resort Destination.

Looking west at a portion of Coeur d'Alene. What was once a rowdy, boom-times logging and lumber town has now become an international resort destination.

An historic shot of the same location, taken in the early 1900s, when the lake served as a hub for flourishing steamboat and sawmill industries. The beauti-ful lake is over 26 miles long and has 100 miles of scenic shoreline. Today, it is a playground for every type of water sport, including cruises featuring everything from bird watching to elegant dinners to day-long scenic excursions.

The Coeur d'Alene Resort,
a World Class Resort in Coeur d'Alene, Idaho.

The award-winning, 18-story, four-star Coeur d'Alene Resort, located on the shore of one of the most beautiful lakefront communities in the West. It features elegant accommodations, excellent cuisine, a rejuvenating and luxurious 30,000 square-foot European spa (newly renovated in 2006), and a Gold Medal golf course with its unique floating green. The resort, built by local resident Duane Hagadone, opened in 1986 amidst much skepticism that anyone would come to this little isolated town. The resort, now among America's top 10, attracts people from all over the world and has given the city of Coeur d'Alene its popular resort identity.

Some of the finest boats in the Inland Northwest are moored at the Coeur d'Alene Resort's marina.

Lunch at the exquisite Beverly's in the Coeur d'Alene Resort includes a spectacular view of the lake.

Checking out the Coeur d'Alene Resort's extensive wine selections with Chris Mueller, the manager of Beverly's.

Beverly's wine steward presenting and uncorking (inset) the wine.

The toast.

Josh Edmondson and his friend Nikesha Thompson, both students of North Idaho College, raising a toast at the Porch Public House at Hayden Lake, Idaho. Josh is one of North Idaho's wrestler standouts. He won the 2006 NJCAA National Wrestling Championship.

Josh's hometown is Medical Lake, Washington. Following his graduation from Medical Lake High School, he entered North Idaho College and was a walk-on to the Cardinal wrestling team, placing third at the 2005 National Junior College Athletic Association tournament in 2005. He wrestles at 184 pounds, and is a physical-education major. Upon graduation from NIC, he plans to attend the University of Tennessee-Chattanooga.

From left: The author with friends Gene Tillman and John Redal at the Coeur d'Alene Inn in Coeur d'Alene, Idaho. Enjoying the evening at the Porch Public House, located next to the golf course at Hayden Lake, Idaho.

A couple enjoying wine while cruising the Spokane River in a famous Stancraft hand-crafted wooden boat, downriver from Lake Coeur d'Alene.

Angelo's Ristorante
in Coeur d'Alene, Idaho

Angelo's on Fourth Street serves some of the best Italian food in the Inland Northwest. It features authentic Old World Italian cuisine made with fresh organic food and brick oven gourmet pizza. Patrons can also enjoy outdoor dining on Angelo's patio or order food to go.

Dinner and . . .

. . . dessert at Angelo's Ristorante.

Angelo Brunson, proprietor of Angelo's Ristorante, and his wife Julie.

The Brix Restaurant and Nightclub
in downtown Coeur d'Alene

The entrance to the Brix at 317 Sherman Avenue.

A toast to good friends and good food at the popular Brix.

Lake Chatcolet and Heyburn State Park at the south end of Lake Coeur d'Alene. It became accessible by boat from Coeur d'Alene Lake in 1907, when the Spokane River was dammed at Post Falls, raising the level of the lake.

Harrison, Idaho, located on the southeastern shore of Lake Coeur d'Alene at the mouth of the Coeur d'Alene River. The quaint little town of Harrison, once a landing for steamers, is now an inviting destination for boaters.

The Hot Rod Cafe
located in Post Falls, Idaho

The Hot Rod Cafe's display at the Wine, Stein and Dine 2006 fund-raising event at Post Falls. The backdrop is an actual photo of the restaurant. It is one of the area's more unique and interesting restaurants, and is located just off Interstate 90 between Spokane and Coeur d'Alene.

Interior shots of the Hot Rod Cafe.

Rob Elder, owner of the Hot Rod Cafe, celebrating a special occasion with some of his employees.

The Wine Rebel checking out the interior of the Hot Rod Cafe.

Basel Cellars,
a Wine Resort in Walla Walla

Basel Cellars, formerly a private estate built in the late 1990s at a cost of over $14 million, became a wine resort in 2002. It is located in the heart of Washington state's Walla Walla Valley. The resort features luxury overnight accommodations for up to 18 guests in the 13,000 square feet of rustic, yet elegant, facility. Basel Cellars produces about 4,000 cases of wine per year, with a focus on Bordeaux-style blends, Syrah and Cabernet Sauvignon.

The Walla Walla Valley was named by *Sunset Magazine* as the "2005 Wine Destination of the Year" and is a four-season destination. More than 60 wineries are in production in the Walla Walla Valley on more than 1,100 acres of land recognized as the third largest Washington State American Viticultural Area (AVA).

Walla Walla is the most historically significant city in Washington. On September 1, 1836, Narcissa Whitman, one of the first white women to settle west of the Rocky Mountains, arrived at the Walla Walla region along with her husband Dr. Marcus Whitman. Here they established the Waiilatpu Mission in an unsuccessful attempt to convert members of the local Cayuse Indian tribe to Christianity. On November 29, 1847, following numerous deaths from a measles epidemic, members of the tribe killed both Dr. and Mrs. Whitman, along with twelve others at the mission in what became nationally known as the Whitman Massacre. Walla Walla was officially incorporated on January 11, 1862. As a result of a gold rush during this decade, the city became the biggest community in Washington Territory. Following this period, agriculture became the city's largest commercial activity. Today, vineyards and wineries are fast becoming Walla Walla's most significant economic mainstay.

A Mini Photo Tour of Basel Cellars Wine Resort.

The pool behind the main lodge.

The tasting room.

A broader view of the tasting room.

The pool room and wine bar.

The main conference room.

The pool room and wine bar.

The theater.

The wine aging room.

Glen and Pam Cloninger enjoying wine outside their summer home on the shores of Lake Coeur d'Alene. Glen is one of the area's most creative architects. As evidenced by this home designed by Glen, his style is unique to the area.

A special wine tasting event at the Wine Rebel's home.

Toasting the photographer on the banks of the St. Joe River in North Idaho.

California Wine Country,
the American mecca of memorable wine-drinking destinations

I grew up in California wine country, which is where I later began my career in the wine business. Although I now conduct business transactions from my homebase in the Inland Northwest, I am still a broker for Grove Street Brokers in Healdsburg, California. So, naturally, when I began to consider what I wanted to put on the cover of my book, I was drawn to my old home territory. Because California has always been the mecca of our domestic wine industry and is where I learned my trade, I felt strongly that I wanted the cover for my book to include a California vineyard or winery. As I began scouting the Dry Creek Valley and Russian River Valley wineries with this goal in mind, I received a welcoming invitation from Fred Peterson of Peterson Winery near Healdsburg. He liked the concept of my book and gave me permission to use any site in his vineyard for my book cover photo shoot. The beautiful location was perfect. Peterson's welcoming attitude contributed to a fun and productive occasion and great backdrop for my cover photo.

Posing with Jeff Libarle in the Grove Street Brokers' warehouse. Jeff, who is the owner of Grove Street, has been my mentor and friend for many years.

Clockwise from top left: The Wine Rebel (right) with Fred Peterson (center), owner of Peterson Winery near Healdsburg, California, and the author's good friend and fellow wine broker, Rick Raffaini (who prefers good Zinfandel); waiting for the perfect lighting to shoot the cover photo; and a perfect pastoral setting at Peterson's Winery.

Wines from Peterson Winery, with Donner Creek in the background.

The Raford House Bed & Breakfast Inn near Healdsburg is in the heart of the Russian River Valley wine country. It was built in 1880, renovated in 1981, and is now listed as a Sonoma County Historical Landmark.

Mill Creek Vineyards and Winery near Healdsburg, California.

The tasting room at the Chateau De Baun, now owned by Kendall-Jackson, north of Santa Rosa.

The award winning Hop Kiln Winery in the Russian River Valley is one of northern California's most beautiful wineries. The Hop Kiln, built in 1905 for drying hops, has been restored and is a National Historic Landmark.

The Domaine Carneros Winery, located on Duhig Road near Napa, California, is a case study in solar energy.

The solar electric system installed at Domaine Carneros is the largest in Napa County. Providing up to 40% of the winery's electricity, it powers production equipment, air conditioning, refrigeration and other operations at the facility.

Completed in May 2003, the solar array generates enough electricity during the daytime to power over 120 homes. The system is an integral part of Domaine Carneros' efforts to help meet the winery's growing electrical energy needs by using clean, renewable energy resources. In addition to integrating solar power, the winery also incorporated a wide range of energy efficient measures, such as building into the hillside, installing skylights and using heavy insulation.

This 120-kilowatt solar system makes innovative use of an unused asset, the facility's roof, to generate power. This solar electric system reduces the winery's annual energy consumption and contributes to a cleaner environment.

It is estimated that over the next 25 years, the solar-generated electricity at this winery will reduce emissions of carbon dioxide by nearly 900 tons. These emission reductions are equivalent to planting almost 260 acres of trees, or not driving 2.3 million miles in the region.

St. Francis Winery & Vineyards, named after Saint Francis of Assisi, is located in the heart of the Sonoma Valley.

A tailgate party on the parking lot of the San Francisco Giant's ball park. from left to right: Chris Biagi, Stretch Strachan and Perry Boaz.

California is famous for both its great vineyards and its mighty redwoods. In the above photo, pas-sengers in a stage coach pass through the Wawona tree in the Mariposa Grove, circa 1897. *(Archival photo, Library of Congress)* The bottom photo shows some old guy having a pull of wine on a fallen redwood in the Redwood Forest of northern California.

A view of Donner Lake from the summit of Donner Pass in the Sierra Nevada.

This statue at Donner Memorial State Park near Truckee, California, was dedicated to those who lost their lives during the harsh winter of 1846-1847 while en route to what was hoped to be a better life in California. A plaque at the site memorializing what became known as the Donner Party Tragedy lists the 42 members of the party who died and the 48 who survived. During these years, people were seeking the rich agricultural lands to homestead. The great California Gold Rush soon followed.

A parting shot of the Wine Rebel in a California vineyard, then back home to North Idaho, where his children and some family friends enjoy a tailgate picnic at Fernan Lake on the outskirts of Coeur d'Alene.

Enjoying a glass of wine in a backyard grape arbor in Eastern Washington.

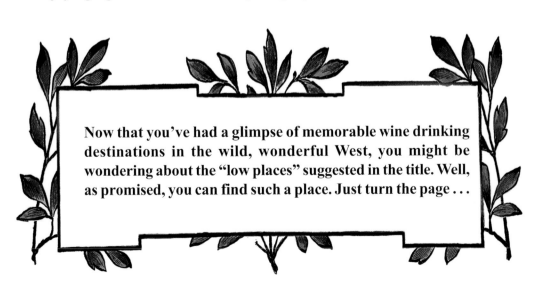

Now that you've had a glimpse of memorable wine drinking destinations in the wild, wonderful West, you might be wondering about the "low places" suggested in the title. Well, as promised, you can find such a place. Just turn the page . . .

This roadside stop outside of Coeur d'Alene, Idaho, would definitely be considered a memorable wine-drinking destination in a low place.

Chapter 9

Wine Myths and Misconceptions

For each wine myth, there is a truth that will easily debunk it and guide your path toward becoming an informed, educated connoisseur. The following are some of the most common wine myths, debunked and explained.

Good Wines Must Be Expensive

Have you ever stood in the aisle of a store looking at two nearly identical bottles of wine with different prices? Your judgment may be telling you to go for the less expensive one, but something inside causes you to hesitate. If they were truly the same quality, wouldn't they be the same price? As you ponder what the hidden differences may be, you convince yourself that the more expensive wine must be worth more and is the better choice. Shouldn't you go with the more expensive one – just to be on the safe side?

Spending big bucks doesn't guarantee a great wine, and spending small bucks does not eliminate the chance of getting good wine. The pricing of wine is somewhat psychological; wines are priced the way they are because people are willing to pay the price, thinking the high price translates into higher quality. A higher-priced wine is perceived to be of higher quality. While this may be true in some instances, it is not the case for most good wines. Unfortunately, the prices on many excellent, lower-priced wines are often raised, lest they be considered inferior to higher-priced wines. The result is an unnecessarily high-priced market where pricier is considered better.

The question to ask yourself is, "What does a $30 wine taste like compared to a $70 wine?" It's often hard to tell the difference, isn't it? The best bet is to compare a few variously priced wines on each end of the price scale. At first, you may want to try these comparisons with your spouse or a friend or even arrange a blind wine tasting party with a number of your friends. After doing this, you'll see what I mean. The best example of price versus quality is the recent "Two Buck Chuck," the name of a new line of California wines sold under the Charles Shaw label. These wines include Cabernet, Merlot, Chardonnay and Sauvignon Blanc, bottled and packaged attractively by the Bronco Wine Company.

When first out, they sold exclusively at Trader Joe's 188 stores for $1.99 a bottle. Two Buck Chuck gained a reputation of being a good inexpensive wine. Initially, there were numerous reports of blind tests comparing it with wines many times its price, with the cheaper wine often the winner. Two Buck Chuck was an exception and was not able to sustain that cost, but it did clearly demonstrate a point I will make more than once. In the world of wine, price does not necessarily equate to quality. In my business, on an almost daily basis, I am constantly amazed at the quality of wines coming from many of the West's small, unknown wineries.

You Must Keep Bottles Protected From the Light

It is a well-known fact that the sun's rays can damage things they come in contact with. They fade furniture, cause plants to wilt and cause sunburns. Wine is no exception. It can also be damaged by the sun's rays. Wine bottles should never be left or stored in direct sunlight.

Another concern I have heard is possible damage caused by natural light or lights in a wine cellar or other types of wine storage facilities. Wine cellars, by nature, tend to be cozy, dark spots where little, if any, direct sunlight penetrates. Temperature is the most important factor in wine storage for long periods of time. Your wine cellar should be between 50 to 58 degrees. It is also important that wine bottles with real corks be stored on their sides. This keeps the corks saturated with wine, preventing them from drying and allowing air to enter the bottle.

Artificial light, such as overhead and side lighting, is neither strong enough nor intense enough to have any sort of effect on wine. There is also a designed advantage to wine bottles. Most wine comes with its own safety feature – the bottle. The dark color of a wine bottle does not come merely from the liquid inside, but also from tinting that is added to the glass. The result is a coat of protection that will keep your wine safe from the effects of casual everyday exposure to light.

Wine Cellars Must Be Kept Humid

A wine cellar does not need to be kept humid unless it stores wine in wooden barrels. The myth that cellars need to be kept humid stems from the days when humidity was, in fact, a necessity to maintain the integrity of the wine. Originally, owners of wine cellars kept their wine in large wooden barrels (most often oak). As a result, the cellars needed to be kept humid to keep the barrels from drying out from the outside. Dry, cold air would suck the moisture from the wood, causing it to shrink and crack. As a result, the wine could seep out or evaporate. Humidity is a factor when wine is kept in barrels. Low humidity in a barrel causes water to evaporate, which tends to concentrate the flavor of the wine. Higher humidity causes alcohol to evaporate faster than water. Because most wine connoisseurs today store their collections in the bottles rather than wooden barrels, humidity is not a concern.

Old Vine Wines Are Better

Older vines often produce smaller yields of grapes that tend to have a higher concentration of flavor; on the other hand, some old vines are simply old and don't produce quality grapes. There is no way to guarantee, based on the age of a vine, if it will produce a quality grape and, therefore, a quality wine. Because different palates enjoy different tastes, it is impossible to say if an older vine is better than a younger vine; just as beauty is in the eye of the beholder, taste is in the palate of the consumer.

Old Wine Is Better Than New Wine

Those who collect wine know the older the bottle, the more expensive it may be. This leads people to believe that because older wines cost more, they taste better. The real reason for the higher interest in older bottles is because older bottles are rarer. However, up to a certain point, prior to the beginnings of deterioration, older wines become smoother.

Wine-savvy people know older wines bring with them a rich history and a bit of romance of years gone by, but what is less known is that with too much aging, they can also bring a deterioration of aromas and flavors. Most people who taste an "aged" wine for the first time are disappointed, because what they are usually getting is, quite simply, an "old" wine.

A Wine With Many "Legs" Is a Higher Quality Wine

Have you ever watched someone handle a freshly poured glass of wine? With a swirl of the wine glass, they will most likely hold it up to see the wine adhere to the side of the glass with what are known as "legs." The more legs you see streaking on the sides of the glass, the better. The idea that wine with legs translates into quality is incorrect. While it may appear impressive to watch for and scrutinize the legs as they run down the insides of you glass, you are actually observing the presence of ethanol, the primary alcohol in wine. Although ethanol is a major contributor to the "body" of a wine, a high content does not alone guarantee fullness or texture in the wine.

Reserve Wines Are Always Superior to Non-reserve Wines

Although reserved wines may be considered excellent by the winemaker, there is no guarantee his/her tastes will match yours. During my career, I have found that reserve wines often are better than non-reserve, but that isn't always the case. Reserve wines can be good examples of high assumed value being applied to a wine specifically because it is labeled "Reserved." One reason why many consumers consider reserve wines to be superior is because they cost more. Most reserve wines are stored for a longer period in the oak barrels, which can be a pricey endeavor that drives the price higher. The best way to determine if a reserve is better than non-reserve is to pop the corks on both bottles and do your own taste test.

Tasting Wine Is Difficult

Very few people are schooled and skilled enough in the wine world to be able to truly tell the differences between wines, or detect flaws within a given bottle. Those that do possess these skills are more often than not the ones who do it for a living and are not necessarily cracking the bottle open over dinner with friends. Therefore, when it comes to tasting wine, comparing different blends and analyzing the flavors you experience, go for something you enjoy. When trying a new wine, take a sip, let it settle into your mouth, and after you have swallowed, decide if you like it or not. Most importantly, don't feel pressure to find hidden flavors (such as creosote) and special meanings in each glass you drink, as most of that type of wine-speak is simply hot air.

Wine tasting rooms are a good way to sample wine varietals and brands that are new to you and have fun while doing so. And, here is an important tip. Typically, the wines offered in tasting rooms are not the wineries' best. Don't hesitate to ask to sample their best wines. But beware. The more wines you sample, the less discerning your palate becomes and the higher your chances become of buying wines you won't enjoy later.

"The Best Wine" Does Exist

No matter how many vineyards, wineries or tasting rooms you visit, or numerous bottles you sample, the truth is that you will not find that one illusive "perfect wine." The best wine is simply the one you like the most. Trying to pick a "best" wine is like trying to decide which one of your children is the "best." It is impossible, because each one (wine and child) has distinctive qualities that you enjoy, and each shines brighter in different situations. You learn to appreciate and love each for their uniqueness. The best way to find your own "best wine" is to sample various types. Note what you appreciate about each, and then venture out looking for new discoveries that will satisfy or excite your palate. You will discover some that are enjoyable, while others are objectionable. The point is, through the

White wine befitting the occasion, an evening in the Isabella Room of the Davenport Hotel.

sampling process, you will become a better judge of what you like. Don't just settle for another's opinion, but choose wines that delight your senses.

White Wine Does Not Age Well

In most cases, white wines age faster and will not last as long as red wines. That does not mean that they will not keep. It just means that you will need to consume them sooner than some of your red wines. Properly stored, white wines typically will last anywhere from two to five years in a wine cellar. As a rule of thumb, high quality chardonnays should be stored no longer than four or five years. Don't think those years spent in storage are all chipping away at the quality of the product; during part of the time spent in storage, white wine will mature and soften, allowing the fruit flavors to become more distinct.

White Wine Must Be Chilled and Served Very Cold

Chilling wine takes away from the detailed character of the flavor; therefore, the colder it is, the less distinct it will taste. Many people go by the rule that white wine should always be chilled. While a quick visit to the refrigerator – 30 to 45 minutes – will allow the wine to cool to the point that it feels good on the throat. Any longer will mask its unique flavors.

Wines Need to be Opened for Long Periods of Time in Order to Breathe Properly and Become Smoother

If you remove the cork from your wine long before you plan on consuming it, you are providing it with a limited opportunity to breathe, which most people believe enables the wine to become smoother and taste better. The real reason for opening a bottle of wine and not immediately pouring it is to allow the aeration process to remove the sulfur smell that may accompany freshly opened bottles. However, in most cases, the best method is to immediately pour it into the glass as soon as the bottle is opened. Because of the wide rims, within 10 to 15 minutes from the time it is poured into a glass, you will notice a difference.

For those who insist the taste of wine changes throughout the course of an evening, consider this: It may be you, rather than the wine, that is undergoing changes. Your first sip may have been on an empty stomach, and your taste buds will respond as they experience the complexity of flavors from both your meal and the wine you consume. The more you consume, the less discerning your taste buds become.

You Must Always Use the Right Wine Glass

In my opinion, there really is no right or wrong glass for wine tasting – or for drinking wine for that matter. However, there are some glasses that are better than others for evaluating wines. The actual size of the glass is not important other than it needs to be big enough, with a circumference wide enough, to be able to easily smell the wine. What difference in taste do you actually think you will find in glasses with a half inch circumference difference?

Wine Is Bad For Your Health

For every person who enjoys the pleasure of a glass of wine, there are others who are quick to list the health risks. Some experts will tell you it is bad for your liver, kills your brain cells and causes drunkenness, which is true if you drink to excess. Limiting your intake and consuming responsibly, however, will not only keep you from harming your health, but may in fact be good for you (see chapter 6).

Shipwreck Wines Are More Complex

Depending on the age of the sunken ship, most old wines found at the bottom of the sea as a result of a shipwreck are not drinkable. Typically, these types of wine are spoiled – smelling of sulfur and rotten eggs. Most of these older wines have been tainted by sulfur-producing bacteria that live at the bottom of the sea.

Collectors of old wines often describe extreme vintage wine as being more complex and collect it as a trophy or status symbol. However, after wine reaches a certain age, it will no longer be palatable. Wine is a fruit-based product and, when fruit passes a certain stage, the so-called complexities of taste these collectors report are, in reality, the flavor of decaying and deteriorating fruit. When it comes to extremely aged wine, it is important to consider that fruit is an organic substance and not immortal. One of the most important objective standards I apply is, that to be great vintage wine, it has to retain some fresh fruit essence. As a basic rule of thumb, wine over 40 years old, even if properly stored, is on the down-hill stretch. To me, wines are truest to their *terroir* in their first ten years of existence.

Many collectors of old wine consider a 50-year-old wine a great trophy. I have tasted wines around that age and have not found them to be great or complex in any manner. Basically, there is nothing special or complex going on with wines that are too old. To me, they simply taste stale, old and tired.

The Other Page to Read

Wine and Food Pairing

The best advice I can give on this almost-inbred, generally accepted concept is – don't do it. If you're enjoying a great steak, lobster or any type of excellent cuisine, I don't think it's in your best interest, taste-wise, to mix it with wine of any color or varietal. In my opinion, doing this seems to take away from the flavor of a good meal. However, this is just my opinion and, if you enjoy food and wine pairing, there are numerous books available on that subject.

Consider this: America is blessed with innumerable master chefs who turn food into paradigms of excellence. The best chefs are typically well schooled and experienced in the art of food and flavor blending. During the preparation of your meal, they will add whatever seasoning they know best complements your specific selection, which may, among other flavorings, include wine. Master chefs create culinary brilliance. What they have prepared should be enjoyed for the quality of its distinctive essence.

In the same context, good vintners are also masters of their trade. Great wines should also be enjoyed for what they are. If the food is great and the wine is great, how can you truly enjoy either if you dilute one with the other? What surprises me is the number of chefs who ascribe to this food pairing nonsense. What chef wouldn't want his or her creation to be enjoyed on its own merit?

I can think of a couple reasons why I would drink wine with food. Either the wine isn't that good and, therefore, having food with it makes the bad wine not so noticeable, or the food isn't good and the wine helps mask what the food is lacking in taste and quality. I suggest you don't go along with the myth – think this one out.

Screw Tops and Wine in a Box

Screw tops and wine in a box may be appropriate for an annual picnic in the park or bingo night, but in my opinion, that's about all. Imagine the wine steward at your favorite restaurant bringing you a boxed wine to inspect or attempting to open a wine bottle's screw-top lid with a flair. To me, popping the cork has, and will always be, a great part of the romance and experience of wine.

Chapter 10

A Brief History of Wine
From Ancient Egypt to the New World

G rapes and their juices are ancient, virtually as old as mankind. In fact, 60-million-year-old fossil vines have been found, which are the earliest prehistoric evidence of grapes. Scientific tests show that wine was produced by man 8,000 years ago.

The initial cultivation of grapes is lost in antiquity. Wild grapes *(vitis vinifera)*, which are now virtually extinct, grew throughout the ancient Mediterranean, and there seems little doubt these were the forerunners of an industry that flourished in Egypt and Greece several thousand years BC. There is dispute about where cultivation originated, but there are indications (possible, but not proven) that Egypt may have been originally responsible. In the earliest pre-dynastic and dynastic periods (3200 BC), vineyards existed for the use of Egypt's rulers and noble families.

Early Egyptian tombs of the first dynasty record the presence of vineyards and wine cellars. Grapevines were first used in formal gardens on large Egyptian estates for their beauty as well as utility; later, they were grown in orchards along with other fruits and vegetables. In addition to vineyards owned by the nobles, the pharaohs cultivated grapes as well, and large vineyards were found on the grounds of the temples. A total of 513 vineyards are listed as belonging to the Temple of Karnack, home of the Egyptian sun god, Amon-Ra. The best vineyards were in the Nile Delta, the Fayyum, Memphis, southern Egypt and the oases. Fairly detailed pictures of them, together with the techniques of wine production were found in Egyptian tombs. The grapes were crushed in vats and pressed by human feet; the juice flowed into smaller

Shesmu, the mythical Egyptian god of precious oils for beauty and embalming, is also a god of the wine press.

vats and finally into pottery jars, where the juice was fermented. It is interesting to speculate on how much experimentation went into the process before the Egyptians discovered this method of making wine from grape juice. No doubt they discovered early on the pleasures to be found in the fermented grape. An ancient Egyptian proverb depicts the following: "In water you see your own face, but in wine the heart of its garden."

One of the most interesting archaeological finds relating to Egyptian wine production came from the tomb of King Tutankhamun, who became king of Egypt at age 10. King Tut reigned for nine years prior to his death about 1323 BC, at the age of 19. On November 4, 1922, King Tut's tomb was discovered by Howard Carter, Chief Inspector of

A group of people at the base of the Great Pyramid in Eygpt, circa 1880. *(Archival photo, Library of Congress)*

Antiquities to the Egyptian Government, and Lord Carnarvon, an English aristocrat who financed the archaeological expedition. The tomb was hidden beneath the mud-brick houses of the workmen who constructed the tomb of Rameses VI. Tut's tomb was not originally carved for a king, but because King Tut died at an early age, the tomb of a high official was hurriedly converted for his use. This inconspicuous location contributed to its protection from grave robbers over the centuries.

This particular tomb is especially significant because it is the only tomb of an Egyptian king to be discovered almost completely undamaged, its contents untouched by thieves. Consequently, it preserved a great record of the culture of the times. Among numerous riches and artifacts found in the tomb were 24 containers of wine that carried labels describing the wine estate, year of vintage and name of the winemaker. On one jar, the inscription reads: "Year 4. Sweet wine of the House-of-Aton-life, prosperity, health – of the Western River, chief vintner Apershop." Another states: "Year 5. Wine of the House-of-Tutankhamun Ruler-of-the-Southern-On, 1.p.h. [in] the Western River. By the chief vintner Khaa."

Egypt was one of the first known civilizations to incorporate wine into its religious traditions as an offering to the gods. Wine was also a symbol of death and rebirth, and considered only for the holy and elite of Egypt. On festive occasions, wine was often consumed by the general public, though, as a general rule, beer was the most popular Egyptian drink among the poor classes.

The Greeks and Romans

The early Greeks also grew grapes. They produced wine and exported it on a large scale. As they moved into Italy, vineyards became even more important. Grapes were cultivated in the south of Italy by Greek colonists and in the north by Etruscans. In the early years of Rome's fight to achieve dominance in the Mediterranean, vineyards and winemaking became secondary in importance. Following Rome's defeat of the Etruscans, Sammites, Greeks and Carthaginians, Rome gained control of the Mediterranean. About this time, the Romans began to realize there was wealth to be had in producing wine for foreign markets.

Shipping from the ancient Athenian harbor at Piraeus, Greece, circa 1907. *(Archival photo, Library of Congress)*

The Temple of Bosco in Rome, Italy, circa 1900. *(Archival photo, Library of Congress)*

In about 160 BC, in one of the earliest surviving pieces of Roman prose, the Roman Marcus Porcius Cato, the Elder, wrote a significant treatise on agriculture (*De Agricultural*) in which he discussed the production of wine on large slave-based villa estates, and stressed the importance of vine cultivation to the economy. By 154 BC, wine production in Italy was unsurpassed. In that year, vine growing was prohibited beyond the Alps, so that during the first two centuries BC, all wine was exported to the provinces, especially to Gaul, in exchange for the slaves whose labor was essential for the large estate vineyards.

By the first century AD, the picture was changing because the demand for wine in Rome was so great. It was necessary to import wine from Spain and other areas. Mulsum, a cheap wine sweetened with honey, was frequently dispensed to the commoners in return for their political support. Even the humblest of hosts felt required to serve wine to all of his guests even though his household budget may have been strained to the limit.

Columella, a first-century Italian who also wrote about agriculture *(De Re Rustica)*, suggested the dregs from the wine press be given to the livestock, "for they contain the strength both of food and of wine and make the cattle sleek and of good cheer and plump." One cannot help but imagine the *good cheer* created in the bovine herds by such largesse.

During the first century, viticulture in the Roman Empire became highly developed, and many of the practices begun at that time are still in use. Many Romans deplored the increased production of cheap wines, and frequently wrote about the importance of maintaining vintage wines that improved with age.

Hauling wine by mule-drawn cart to Rome from the Frascati vineyards in Italy, circa 1904. *(Archival photo, Library of Congress)*

Vineyard in Montal Pruno New Staggia in Chianti, Italy, in 2005. *(Photo courtesy David Brubaker and Kaye Adkins)*

A view of Staggia and its vineyards from Montzeprimo, Italy. *(Photo courtesy David Brubaker and Kaye Adkins)*

Distillation was unknown in the ancient world and was not discovered until the early middle ages, so wine was the strongest drink available to the Romans and to the world in general.

Falernian, the most highly prized wines at that time, had an alcohol content of 15 or 16 percent, and although it was a white wine, it became the color of amber when aged for 10 to 20 years.

Wine was almost always mixed with water for drinking, as undiluted wine was considered a drink used only by provincials and barbarians. It was also realized, during those times, that wine had a purifying effect. Romans usually mixed one part wine to two parts water (sometimes even sea water). The Greeks were more inclined to dilute their wine with three or four parts water and drank with the intention of enjoying the aesthetic pleasure of the wine, becoming intoxicated just enough to indulge in stimulating conversation and to have the mind released from inhibition. Their Roman counterparts had a tendency to get more blatantly drunk.

On August 24, 79 AD, Mount Vesuvius erupted and its ash preserved for eternity Roman life as it was lived in Pompeii, a small city near the Bay of Naples in Italy. At the time, Pompeii was estimated to have a population of about 20,000. A study of the gods and goddesses worshiped in Greek and Roman mythology indicate some of the same values and customs that are reflected in our western culture today.

Dionysius, also known as Bacchus, the Greek and Roman god of wine, with Pan the half-goat, half-human patron god of shepherds and flocks. *(This was the first sculpture done by Michelangelo, 1497.)*

According to mythology, Dionysus was born from the thigh of Zeus, the supreme ruler of the gods. After his birth, Dionysus, or Bacchus as he was called in ancient Greece, was raised by the nymphs who lived on the mythical Mount Nysa, where he spent his childhood and planted the first grapevine. After reaching adulthood, he traveled through Asia Minor, the Middle East and the Mediterranean, teaching people the art of growing grapes for wine. He was also generally considered the god of fertility.

Wine drinking flourished in Pompeii. Wine prices were posted throughout the city, and varied according to the quality of the wine. One sign can still be read: "For one 'asses' [a Roman coin] you can drink wine; for two, you can drink the best; for four you can drink Falernian." (A loaf of bread cost two asses.) Some 200 drinking establishments have been found in Pompeii, many near the public baths. Pliny writes of the residents and their attempt to acquire a thirst. "First," he says, "they went to the baths, getting so hot as sometimes to become unconscious, then rushing out, often still naked, to grab a large vessel of wine at an outdoor *thermopolium* [the fast food and drink establishment of the day] and swill down its contents, only to vomit it up again so more could be drunk."

In 212 AD, citizenship was conferred on all free male inhabitants of the Roman Empire and, in 280 AD the edict that had prohibited vine growing in the provinces was revoked, thereby eliminating the exclusivity of the privilege of cultivating vines, which previously had been the prerogative only of Roman citizens. With everyone in the provinces now permitted to grow wine grapes, wine culture was free to develop in France, Germany, Spain and other regions of the Roman Empire.

The Bible

One of the earliest vintners on record was Noah, who, at an advanced age, loaded his wife, sons, their wives, and an assortment of earthly creatures into his ark and survived a great flood. He then became a husbandman and planted a vineyard – on one occasion, at least, becoming drunk as a result. The Old Testament frequently mentions vineyards and wine, sometimes as used in ceremonies, but frequently as a part of everyday life. King David, after bringing the Ark of the Covenant into Jerusalem, gave everyone in the whole multitude of Israel "a cake of bread, a good piece of meat, and a flagon of wine." The writer of the lovely Song of Solomon avows several times: "For thy love is better than wine."

Although the Bible contains warnings about the dangers of overimbibing in wine and strong drink, and the resultant drunkenness, wine was an accepted part of daily life. Verses emphasizing the more positive aspects of wine drinking are frequent and are often connected with the blessings of God. Some excerpts follow:

Be no longer a drinker of water, but use a little wine for thy stomach's sake. *(1 Timothy 5:23)*

That he may bring forth food out of the earth and wine that maketh glad the heart of man. *(Psalms 104:14-15)*

And God give thee of the dew of heaven, and of the fatness of the earth, and plenty of grain and new wine. *(Genesis 27:28)*

... Jehovah thy God will keep with thee the covenant ... he will bless thee and will bless the fruit of thy ground, thy grain and thy new wine ... *(Deuteronomy 7:12-13)*

Leonardo da Vinci's painting of the *Last Supper*, one of the world's most renowned and appreciated masterpieces, depicts the last gathering of Jesus Christ and his disciples. According to the *Bible*, this last supper included bread and wine. Two references from the Life Application Bible specifically address the usage of wine during the last supper.

Matthew 26:27 *And he took a cup of wine and gave thanks for it and gave it to them and said, "Each one of you drink from it, for this is my blood, sealing the New Covenant. It is poured out to forgive the sins of the multitudes. Mark my words—I will not drink this wine again until the day I drink it with you in my Father's Kingdom."*

Mark 14:22-24 *As they were eating, Jesus took bread and asked God's blessing on it and broke it in pieces and gave it to them and said, "Eat it–this is my body." Then he took a cup of wine and gave thanks to God for it and gave it to them; and they drank from it. And he said to them, "This is my blood poured out for many, sealing the new agreement between God and man. I solemnly declare that I shall never again taste wine until the day I drink a different kind in the Kingdom of God."*

A search of the *New International King James* version of the *Bible* produced 228 references to wine, 58 of which refer to its use as a cultural norm 27 to wine as a blessing from God, 19 to the loss of wine as a curse from God, 9 refer to it as a gift between people, and 13 references address warnings of its abuse.

Many of the stories of Jesus also involve wine. For the marriage in Cana of Galilee, he turned water into wine at his mother's request – one of the early miracles that convinced Jesus's disciples of his divinity. Certainly wine was a significant and integral part of the last supper, an event that has sustained Christianity throughout the ages.

The Middle Ages (ninth to eleventh centuries)

Despite the many regulations imposed by Rome during its golden years, vine cultivation spread northward into Gaul (now France) and Germany and even into Britain, and although wine making was somewhat restricted by climate in those areas, the advancement of viticulture continued and eventually flourished. Much of this was accomplished by the efforts of various Roman Catholic religious orders whose members took care to protect the grapevines and keep the art of wine making alive.

In France, the climate and geography make it unique and, in many ways, perfect for growing grapes. The growing season is long, not too hot, with just the right amount of rainfall. Since much of the soil is porous, good drainage is provided for the vines. Many centuries of research and experimentation have taught the French which grapes grow best in each particular area. Many of these have not changed significantly over the centuries. For example, Bordeaux still produces Cabernet Sauvignon, Merlot, Semillon and Muscadelle. Burgundy is noted for its Chardonnay, Pinot Noir, and Gamay. The Loire Valley claims Sauvignon Blanc and Chenin Blanc.

The Champagne area of France is of special interest, and was a region of national importance long before the introduction of sparkling wine. It lies at the crossroads of northern Europe and, thus, was the setting of many dramatic events in the development of France as a nation. While this location led to repeated destruction, it also brought trade. The medieval powers in the area encouraged commerce, which gave the wines of Champagne easy exposure and access to important wine markets. When the cathedral at Reims was chosen as the coronation site for the French king Hugh Capet in 987 A.D., the city and its monasteries cooperated to make wine production a truly successful endeavor until the 17th century, when champagne, as we know it, was first produced. The cool climate of the region and its effect on the wine making process eventually created the beverage that now defines the area.

Northern Europe

There were few advances in the art of making wine between 400 and 1200 A.D. The monasteries were of the greatest importance in keeping the vines productive, and later the nobility owned extensive vineyards. From the 13th century forward, wines from Bordeaux were typically shipped to England, the Hanseatic ports of northern Germany, and the Low Countries of Belgium, Flanders and the Netherlands.

Of note, Germany, the most northerly of the wine-growing countries, has for centuries had the distinction of producing the lightest and most delicate white wines in the world, wines that are low in alcohol and delightfully balanced. Attempts by other regions to duplicate these wines have not been notably successful, especially the Rieslings. Soil structure, climate and the practice of harvesting grapes at various degrees of ripeness all contribute greatly to the unique character of these German wines. After the Fall of the Roman Empire, it was Germany's many monastic orders, and their meticulous care of the vines and wines, that preserved the country's wine culture. They set the standard for the high quality of German viticulture.

The British Isles

What was happening in England during these medieval years? Although England never became as intensely active as France and Germany in the production of wine, the English had been introduced to the juice of the grape by the Romans, who felt they were pre-destined to spread the pleasures of wine throughout their empire. Generally, ale was a more popular drink in England, but the *Domesday Book* of 1086 mentions 45 vineyards that belonged to both monasteries and private parties in the country. There is evidence that when William the Conqueror arrived on England's shore in 1066, he brought wine with him and his troops. The Bayeux Tapestry, which depicts the great events of William's conquest, includes pictures of wine casks being hauled by horse-drawn wagons. Whether the wine was for the benefit of the conquered Englishmen or for William's troops from Normandy, or both, is not clear.

By about mid-1100, William of Malmesbury praised the wines produced in the valleys of Gloucester as follows:

> In this region the vines are thicker, the grapes more plentiful and their flavor more delightful than any other part of England. Those who drink this wine do not have to purse their lips because of the sharp and unpleasant taste, indeed it is little inferior to French wine in sweetness.

The New World

Students of viticulture, and its arrival in what was to become America, need to consider Leif Erickson's possible contribution. Erickson was supposedly born about 980, perhaps in Iceland. So many legends have grown around him that he has become almost Arthurian in reputation. A tale is told in the *Icelandic Sagas,* a body of medieval Icelandic literature, that on one of his journeys he found a land where grapes grew, which he later called Vineland (or wine land), which may have been Newfoundland.

Columbus arrived in the New World in 1492 and the provisions aboard his ship included the following liquids: water, vinegar, wine, olive oil, and molasses. The olive oil was stored in earthenware jugs; the other items in wooden casks. There is no evidence to suggest that he carried vines or any other plant life, and no mention is made whether or not he found wine produced by the native people.

The Pilgrim passengers aboard the *Mayflower* probably had beer to drink and perhaps wine, because it was almost impossible to keep fresh water on such a lengthy voyage, and wine is far more resistant to bacteria than water. Of interest to historians, the *Mayflower* was a cargo ship of 180-ton capacity and had served the wine trade between France and England for many years before her voyage to the New England coast.

As the British colonies in North America became more populated, all types of alcoholic beverages became available. Since distillation was now common, rum and whiskey, as well as beer and wine were prevalent. Alcoholic beverages were also made from such things as tomatoes, onions, dandelions, corn silk and goldenrod. In early America, most colonies required the towns to license suitable persons to deal in spirits.

The more wealthy landowners in America brewed or distilled their own beverages. Taverns were common in every town and were often located near the church or meetinghouse. Court sessions were frequently held in major taverns in various colonial towns.

Benjamin Franklin, the spokesman for the common man who had something to say about everything, had plenty to say about wine and drinking. Some favorite quotes are:

> There cannot be good living where there is not good drinking.

> Wine makes daily living easier, less hurried, with fewer tensions and more tolerance.

> Take counsel in wine, but resolve afterwards in water.

He also provided us with his own version of the story of Noah (somewhat different from that of the Old Testament), which brings us full circle in our discussion of the history of wine and wine making:

> Before Noah, men having only water to drink, could not find the truth. Accordingly… they became abominably wicked, and they were justly exterminated by the water they loved to drink. This good man, Noah, having seen that all his contemporaries had perished by this unpleasant drink, took a dislike to it; and God, to relieve his dryness, created the vine and revealed to him the art of making "le vin." By the aid of this liquid he unveiled more and more truth.

Chapter 11

Great American Wine Country

There have always been native grapes in North America that were hardy enough to withstand the extremes in climate so typical of most of the continent. Cultivation of grapes into wine-producing crops began with efforts to claim and settle lands in the New World. The problem faced by early colonists, many of whom would have been quite willing to produce wine, was that wine from the native grapes didn't have a pleasing taste and was disappointingly inferior to the European wines 17th century people were accustomed to.

Early attempts to transplant European grapes to American soil were unsuccessful and, although settlers in all the colonies tried to grow the European *Vitis vinifera* vines, the results were almost always disappointing. The *vinifera* grapes that produced the excellent wines of Europe not only were vulnerable to the unfavorable American climate, they also had no immunity to the various diseases or pests to which they were exposed, especially the devastating phylloxera, a plant louse that attacks the roots of the vines and destroys the plants. Native American vines were immune to these parasites. How the problem was discovered and solved is a fascinating story of its own. Without going into all the lengthy details, it is important to recognize what was finally achieved by vintners who grafted the *vinifera* vines to the hardy native American rootstock with no loss in quality of the grapes produced. This process didn't occur overnight. It was accomplished over a long period by many people who truly cared about improving the state of American wine production.

At the present time, the United States ranks as the world's fourth largest wine producing nation in the world. In the last 25 years, wine consumption in America has increased by almost 400 percent and, as people become more educated about its health benefits, it is expected to continue climbing. Every state in the union has at least a couple of wineries and, as a result of the wine culture's growing popularity and the related tourist trade, many states are actively developing or expanding their wine production enterprises.

The following is a brief overview of how the wine industry developed in some of the more successful viticulture areas from the East Coast to the Midwest and, nearly simultaneously, in the southwestern part of the country.

East of the Rockies

Virginia

Virginia and the London Company led the way in Early America toward encouraging the planting of vineyards. The early settlers had high expectations for the financial benefits that would derive from producing wine and shipping it to European markets. Their hopes were not realized, but viticulture continued in the colony. Repeated attempts to transplant European grapes on American soil proved futile, as much of the North American climate was harsher than that of France, the Mediterranean area and even Germany. Though hardier, and more capable of surviving the extremes of temperatures, the native grapes produced wine that was not palatable. Despite the many difficulties, however, Virginia vintners were successful in growing some hybrid varieties that are still in existence today, such as the Alexander, Norton, Catawba and others.

Thomas Jefferson was a wine connoisseur and an ardent advocate for promoting the wine industry. Although hard liquor was the customary drink in his day, Jefferson believed wine was a healthier beverage. Jefferson was known to have consistently imported vast amounts of wine from France.

During the Civil War, a substantial number of vineyards in the East were devastated by disease and neglect due to the reduced labor force, as a tremendous number of the region's young men were enlisted in the Union and Confederate armies. Virginia's vineyards did not recover for many years following the war. By 1900 there were almost none left in the state. However, by 1960, Virginia saw a rebirth of wine making, due in large part to the growing national desire for and interest in wines. Thanks to enterprising grape growers and favorable laws, and with the help of Virginia Tech and the Virginia Wine Growers Advisory Board, Virginia has shown a remarkable upsurge in production. As a testament to the adaptability and willingness of Americans to work with prevailing conditions, Virginia now produces wines that receive national and international acclaim, made from grapes that vary tremendously from the eastern shore to the mountainous western area of the Blue Ridge.

Florida

The Sunshine State has an ancient link to wine making, as its wild grapes were found in abundance by the Spanish a century before the *Mayflower* reached American shores. Muscadine wine is especially important here because its aromatic and smooth qualities are found nowhere else in the world. With hybridization, its quality has been consistently improved. The University of Florida is dedicated to producing and improving Florida's grapes, and the future of the industry in all areas of the state is promising. The wine industry is an aspect of Florida that is appealing to many people, especially tourists in search of new ways to relax amidst such an accommodating industry.

New York

New York's wine history dates back to when the Dutch settled New York and planted the first grapevines during the first half of the 17th century, most of which did not survive. New York's Hudson Valley claims the oldest continuously operating winery in the United States, the Brotherhood Winery. It was established in 1839 and managed to survive Prohibition by producing medicinal and sacramental wines sanctioned by the government.

The state of New York is the nation's third largest wine producer behind California and Washington. Geographically, it encompasses a variety of climates and topography favorable for growing grapes. During the Ice Age, New York was heavily glaciated, leaving much of the state with deep, fertile, though somewhat rocky, soils. The glaciers also left numerous swampy areas that created rich humus soils, which are perfect for various agricultural purposes. Today, the major wine producing areas span the width of the state, and include the Hudson River region, the Finger Lakes in central New York, Long Island on the coast, and along the shores of Lake Erie. According to a governor's press release in June 2006, there are about 185 wineries in the state, which produce nearly 200 million bottles of wine annually. It is an industry that exceeds $420 million and attracts 4 million tourists annually.

New Jersey

Wine making became a tradition in New Jersey during colonial times, well over 200 years ago. The Atlantic winds create a moderate climate, and the terrain consists of both hillsides and lowlands with good sun exposure that are suited to growing grapes. Vineyards planted in the 1760s were the first to begin producing quality wine in the New World worthy of recognition. In 1767, two New Jersey vintners received awards from London's Royal Society of the Arts for their success in producing the first bottles of quality wine made from colonial agriculture. Today, there are about two dozen wineries in the state, including the Renault Winery founded in 1864, making it one of America's oldest operating wineries.

A notable New Jersey claim is the development of grape juice. Dr. Thomas B. Welch, a dentist from Vineland (named for its many vineyards), who was a devout Christian and staunch prohibitionist, objected to the use of alcohol in communion services. In 1869, he discovered a method of pasteurizing grape juice to stop fermentation and produced "Dr. Welch's Unfermented Wine," which he promoted as a suitable alternative for sacramental communion. Though not widely accepted for that purpose, it marked the beginning of the processed fruit juice industry. Charles E. Welch continued his father's pursuit, but with a different focus. He promoted the sale and consumption of grape juice as a desirable beverage, and founded Welch's Grape Juice Company. His big break was at the 1893 Chicago World's Fair, where thousands sampled his juice. Charles left his own dentistry practice to devote his attention to the production of grape juice. Because Concord and Niagara are the most popular grapes for juice, this new market was responsible for the preservation of many vineyards of those varietals during Prohibition (in effect nationally from 1920 to 1933).

Ohio and Indiana

The first successful commercial wine production in the United States was from Cape grapes planted by a group of Swiss immigrants at present day Vevay, Indiana, in the early 1800s. Although numerous other vineyards had been planted earlier in various parts of the United States, the survival rate was extremely bleak. However, the Cape grapes survived, and the first commercial winery was established in 1803. So many vineyards were planted along both banks of the Ohio River from Cincinnati, Ohio, to Louisville, Kentucky, the region became known as the Rhineland of America. It was the center of the American wine industry until the vineyards were decimated by a blight in the 1850s.

In the 1820s, Catawba grapes were planted around the Cincinnati area, where a popular light semisweet wine was produced. The region soon became known for the first sparkling wines produced in America. By 1860, Ohio was the leading wine producer in the country, but the vineyards suffered greatly during the Civil War.

Following the war, German immigrants brought renewed vigor to grape production in Ohio, but their activities centered farther north along the shores of Lake Erie. This area proved to be well suited for growing grapes; the breezes off the lake cool the vineyards in the summer and protect them from colder temperatures in the late fall and early winter. With the unique lake climate and their proven German wine-making techniques, the settlers began producing some excellent wines. Wineries began popping up along the entire southern shore of Lake Erie, which became known as the "Lake Erie Grape Belt." In the 1880s, the Golden Eagle Winery on Lake Erie's Middle Bass Island became the largest wine producer in the country. Because the main varieties grown in this region are Concord and Niagara grapes, popular for making grape juice, many of the vineyards survived Prohibition.

Ohio experienced a resurgence in wine production by the 1960s and is now among the ten top producing states. The Small Winery Act of 1971 revitalized Indiana's wine industry.

Michigan

The viticulture along the shores of Lake Erie in Ohio spread around the west end of the lake into southern Michigan. These vineyards also weathered Prohibition better than some because the main variety grown was the Concord grape. By 1900, Concord grapes had become the basis for both grape juice and wine production, and today, Michigan is one of the top grape producers for the grape juice industry.

Southern Michigan continues to produce about half of the state's wine grapes but vineyards and wineries around Grand Traverse Bay in northern Michigan are becoming more successful every year. Michigan is fortunate to have a viable and influential Grape and Wine Industry Council, and also enjoys the support of Michigan State University's agricultural expertise.

Missouri

The Louisiana Purchase of 1803 created the initial interest in Missouri and settlers came in such numbers that the territory achieved statehood in 1821. Most of the early pioneers were German, but later Swiss, French, Austrians and Italians took advantage of the availability of affordable land. Vineyards soon followed. Land between St. Louis and Jefferson City along the Missouri River, known as Missouri's Rhineland, was especially suitable for grape growing. The German settlement of Hermann was established at the center of this wine country and, according to an article in the *Chicago Tribune* on May 8, 2000, its Stone Hill Winery overlooking the town was at one time the third largest winery in the world (the largest being in Europe and the second largest in Ohio). By 1848, there were enough successful vineyards to hold a grape harvest festival. Their most successful grape was the Norton, one of the oldest cultivated native American grapes, a red variety favored by the Germans. Missouri wines soon began surpassing European wines, winning gold medals in international competitions. It was soon producing as much as 1.25 million gallons of wine a year to meet the demand.

Following the destruction of many of the vineyards in the eastern states during the Civil War, Missouri became the number one wine producer in the country. However, Prohibition brought Missouri wine production to a halt. Over 100 wineries closed and vineyards were left to decay. Assisted by the Missouri Wine Advisory Board and the Fruit Experiment Station at Southwest Missouri State University, the state's wine industry began making a comeback. The Stone Hill Winery, which had closed during Prohibition and was later used for a mushroom-growing operation, reopened in 1965. Not only is it producing wine again, but it's also a popular tourist attraction.

Texas

The history of wine making in Texas, which began with the Spanish missionaries, is hundreds of years old. The Franciscan padres planted wine grapes in the El Paso area in the 1660s,

This drawing, circa 1846, was an attack on the Mexican clergy, who, with their treasures, were deserting Matamoras, the Mexican town on the Rio Grande taken by American troops in May 1846, at the start of the Mexican War. Their "treasures" included young women and wine. A priest and a monk on horseback, with a woman seated behind each, are in the lead. Two more horses with clerics and more women are not far behind. The artist's characterization of the priests as "rulers" was an anti-Catholic attack, alluding to the power of the Church, which was closely allied to wealthy landowners. *(Drawing, Library of Congress)*

but many varieties of wild grapes also flourished. Prior to Prohibition, Texas was a leader in North American viticulture. There were over 20 commercial wineries by the early 1900s, but Prohibition forced them all to close. The state's vineyards and wineries continue to grow, both in production and reputation, and today Texas is the nation's fifth largest wine producer. This huge state has many areas that comprise the Texas wine centers, but the largest concentration is the Texas Hill Country north and west of Austin and San Antonio.

The West Coast

Washington and Oregon

The Pacific Northwest states of Idaho, Oregon and Washington (among others) historically began their existence as one United States territory, and are geographically similar with mountain ranges, forests and dry interior plains. Both Oregon and Washington have a western coastline with a wet, temperate climate that is bordered by the sizable Cascade

Range. Many of the Cascade peaks are among the highest in the continental United States. The more barren land east of the Cascades is far different, with drier climates and soils that require irrigation to produce well. Both states have a network of fertile river valleys of great importance to the wine industry. In Oregon, which includes the Willamette, Rogue and Umpqua rivers, as well as the Columbia River which winds through Eastern Washington from Canada to Oregon (known as the Great Columbia River Basin). At the Oregon border, the Columbia flows west to the Pacific Ocean, serving as the dividing line between Washington and Oregon.

A 1902 photograph of a young woman wearing a wreath of grape leaves and grapes. I like to think of this photo as symbolic to the early West Coast grape industry. *(Archival photo by Fritz W. Guerom, Library of Congress)*

Grapevines were first planted in Washington in 1824 at Fort Vancouver on the Columbia River and, in Oregon, about 1847 in the Willamette Valley by settlers who crossed the Oregon Trail. By the 1850s, wine grapes were being planted in southern Oregon and, the following decade, in the Walla Walla area of southeastern Washington. Now vast tracts of former sagebrush desert are covered with vineyards, and every year more land is converted to viticulture. Washington has seen many of its established apple orchards, for which the state is famous, turned into vineyards.

Numerous American Viticulture Areas (AVAs) have been established throughout Washington and Oregon, the first of which, the Yakima Valley appellation, was formed in 1983. It was followed the next year by Oregon's Willamette Valley and the Walla Walla AVA, which includes land in both Washington and Oregon. Later in the year, the Columbia Valley AVA, Washington's largest, was approved, which included both the Yakima and Walla Walla viticultural areas.

The Walla Walla area is Washington's premier wine country, boasting over 60 wineries with as many vineyards. Oregon's largest wine region, where the majority of the wineries are located, stretches over 100 miles through the Willamette Valley from Portland to Eugene (west of Interstate 5). Its low rolling hills, cool climate and excellent soil make it among the top wine growing regions in the world. Pinot Noir and Pinot Blanc are the favorite grapes grown in the valley, with a waiting list of wineries competing for the fruit. Both states also have other areas of productive vineyards and wineries. In Washington, about 99 percent of the wine produced is from east of the Cascades.

Washington's oldest and most acclaimed winery, Chateau Ste. Michelle, began under another name the year after Prohibition was repealed in 1933, and has some of the most mature vineyards in the Columbia Valley. The winery's headquarters, where they make their white wines, are now located in a picturesque French-style chateau in Woodinville (15 minutes from Seattle). The property was originally the summer home of Seattle lumber baron Frederick Stimson and their residence, listed on the National Register of Historical Places, still graces the winery grounds today. The 87 acres of beautifully landscaped grounds were designed by the Olmsted Brothers, a renowned Massachusetts landscape firm.

Today, Washington and Oregon are the second and fourth (respectively) highest ranking wine-producing states in the country. In number of bonded wineries (meaning they have their own physical plant for producing wine, generally from their own vineyard), Washington ranks second in the county with about 320 and Oregon ranks third with about 230. The production rate and number of wineries (especially those termed "virtual wineries" that do not have their own production facilities) are growing at such a brisk rate that statistics are in a constant state of flux. Generally, what this means is that these two states are extremely well suited to productive viticulture that produces great, award-winning wines. Even the *Vitis vinifera* that was such a colossal disappointment for the colonists on the East Coast grows relatively trouble-free. In addition, the scenic beauty of the widely diverse Pacific Northwest topography readily lends itself to capitalizing on popular winery tourism.

What is especially interesting about the suitability of the Pacific Northwest for excelling in the wine industry is how late viticulture actually became established in this region. Although there is evidence of grapes having been planted in the early to mid-1800s, wine production was fairly hit-and-miss until the second half of the 20th century. The main reason was the delayed settlement in this part of the country and its relative isolation, coupled with the relatively short period of time between settlement and Prohibition. But, the success of the relatively young wine industry in the Pacific Northwest, plus the economic value of grape crops (the highest value fruit crop in the nation), ensures continued growth and development.

Idaho

Idaho, my home state, is often considered the forgotten state in the Pacific Northwest, but it has an early history of wine production. Royal Muscadines were grown as early as 1862, as evidenced by news stories of that era in *The Idaho Statesman.* It reported that vines were planted in the Clearwater Valley by some German and French immigrants, who were credited with bringing cuttings from Europe. Their expertise paid off and Idaho soon developed a nationally renowned, award-winning wine industry that lasted until Prohibition took its toll, as it did everywhere. Idaho's statewide ban on the production of liquor went into effect in January 1917, three years earlier than the national ban, and wasn't repealed until 1935. Viticulture began anew in the 1970s in Idaho, with the majority of the vineyards located along the Snake River Valley in the southwestern part of the state. Plantings continue at a faster pace than ever before in Idaho, and there are now about two dozen wineries.

This grape harvest scene in California depicts, along with other activities, Chinese laborers and other workers hauling baskets, crushing grapes with their feet, and pressing with a large wine press, circa 1880. *(Archival painting, Library of Congress)*

California, America's Greatest Wine Producer

Volumes have been written about the California wine industry and, even with the rapid growth and stellar performances of other states, California remains the undisputed leader in the field, with no threat of losing its position in the foreseeable future. To put this in perspective, California still produces a considerably higher percentage of wine grapes and domestic wine than all of the other 49 states combined. Although Washington and Oregon boast the next highest number of bonded wineries in the country, according to recent statistics in *Wine Business Monthly*, their combined numbers only equal one-third of the number in California. Plus, California has perfected the formula for capitalizing on and promoting wine tourism. Much of this has to do, quite simply, with its years of experience.

The first vineyards in California were planted by the Spanish Franciscan missionaries at their network of 21 missions built between 1769 and 1823. The most notable of the Franciscans was Father Junipero Serra, who founded the first mission in 1769, followed by eight others that stretched from San Diego to San Francisco. Father Serra's influence on what is now the state of California cannot be overemphasized, not only in terms of religion, but also in regards to the economic and political impact. He is said to have brought grains, fruits and vines with him, and has been credited by some as being the "father" of the California wine industry. A bicentennial anniversary of the presumed planting of the first vines was celebrated in 1969. However, scholars have refuted this claim, primarily because his diaries do not mention vines and reflect an ongoing challenge of securing communion wine, clearly indicating he did not have vineyards that produced wine. However, vineyards were planted at the missions and, typically with the aid of Native American labor, they began producing wine shortly before the 71-year-old Father Serra died in 1784.

In 1946, the state of California officially named Agoston Haraszthy as the "father" of its wine industry because of his impact on today's industry. His influence involved introducing a great diversity of varietals from Europe to an otherwise Mission-grape dominated environment, being the first to initiate grand scale vineyards (having planted extensive vineyards for himself and for other landowners) and volume wine production, introducing the concept of blending wines, and being the first winemaker from the area to publish a treatise on the California wine industry. However, in the excellent, well-documented book *A History of Wine in America: From the Beginnings to Prohibition,* author Thomas Pinney makes a good argument that some of the claims made in favor of Haraszthy are rather ill founded, especially in light of a history of viticulture in California that spanned three-quarters of a century prior to his arrival in 1849. As mentioned, the missions had already been producing wine for four decades, and had established techniques and practices followed by future California winemakers. In the 1830s, a group of French immigrants had begun planting commercial vineyards using better quality European grape varieties. It appears that Haraszthy was a self-promoting, enterprising individual, but apparently his influence on today's wine industry seemed worthy enough of the title. The Haraszthy Buena Vista in Sonoma, which he started, is one of the state's oldest existing wineries.

The demand for wine increased with the great influx of people during the California gold rush of the 1850s, and it wasn't long before these California immigrants awakened to the realization that the soil and climate held promises of riches far greater than gold nuggets.

Chinese laborers picking grapes at the J. de Barth Shorb Vineyards, San Marino, California, circa 1880. *(Archival photo, Library of Congress)*

The agricultural potential was huge. Most of the state of California is well suited to growing grapes of one variety or another, but also has all the right elements to grow just about anything, and soon became the top agricultural producer in the nation. Even with the typical cycles inherent in agricultural endeavors, due to such elements as weather, disease, insects and politics, California wineries flourished well into the 20th century. The enactment of Prohibition caused a major setback in the California wine industry, and many vineyards were plowed under to make way for more profitable agricultural enterprises. However, its recovery in such a relatively short time has been nothing short of phenomenal. The primary wine country is north of San Francisco, stretching throughout Sonoma, Napa, Lake and Mendocino counties. In 2005, a record harvest pushed this region's wine grape crop to over $1 billion, a 47% increase over 2004, and the potential in California is still wide open.

Some of the wines represented by Grove Street Brokers of Healdsburg, California.

California's Wine Queens and
a Profile of the 1961 National Wine Queen

It is typical of annual festivals of all kinds to have a queen to reign over the festivities, and in the 1950s and '60s (maybe even as early as the 1940s), a wine queen represented California during National Wine Week. This annual October event centered around the California State Fair in Sacramento, during which California vintners chose a beautiful young woman to act as the wine industry's ambassador to reign over the week-long festivities and, most importantly, pose for stunning publicity photos. This was an important stimulus for the California wine industry and an example of marketing strategy that catapulted California into the number one wine producer in the country. Very little has been written about this tradition, which disappeared sometime in the late 1960s.

The following is a narrated pictorial profile of the late Anne (Henderson) Anderson, the 1961 National Wine Queen. Anne was born on August 2, 1939, in Sacramento, California, and moved to Spokane, Washington, with her family when she was six. While a college student, she won the Miss Washington contest. In 1960, Anne moved back to California, where she pursued a successful modeling career, becoming one of the top models in San Francisco. In 1961, she was chosen National Wine Queen and promoted California wines at numerous wine tastings, luncheons and other affairs.

Anne Henderson being crowned the 1961 National Wine Queen by California Governor and Mrs. Edmund Brown at a ceremony held in San Francisco, and standing beside her official National Wine Queen car. As National Wine Queen, Anne acted as hostess for the California wine growers during the National Wine Week in October. *(Bamonte archival photo from the Anne Henderson/Anderson collection)*

Anne Henderson during the celebration of National Wine Week, which took place October 15-22, 1961.

The actor Jack Kelly, from the famed television show *Maverick*, being served champagne in a silver tasting cup by Anne Henderson, National Wine Queen.

Anne offering a toast (left) and promoting various California wines.

These photos were taken during the three-day Napa Valley Wine Festival in 1958. Lynne (Mrs. Philip) Champlin (top photo, raising a toast) was selected as its queen to reign over the festivities.

Chapter 12

Prohibition, Temperance and Art Depicting the Evils of Drinking Alcohol Beverages to Excess

History is one of the best purveyances of knowledge concerning alcoholic over-indulgence. Centuries before our society confronted the abuse of alcohol, scholars and artists often reflected the problems of their times in writings or, as illustrated in this chapter, artwork. As our nation evolved, the United States attempted to control this problem through the complete prohibition of alcohol. This chapter provides a short summary of Prohibition during the last century, and a brief glance of some early artwork related to the abuse of alcohol.

Prohibition disrupted, but did not destroy, the wine industry in the United States. The Eighteenth Amendment to the Constitution, prohibiting the manufacture, sale, import or export of intoxicating beverages, was passed in 1919. However, before this national amendment, many states and localities already had their own "Dry Laws" in place thanks largely to the temperance movement, particularly the efforts of the Woman's Christian Temperance Union and the Anti-Saloon League. These groups had strong backing from the more conservative Protestant churches, who were especially appalled by working men squandering their earnings on alcohol, while their children went without basic necessities. Even some in the tavern business were concerned. Spokane tavern owner Jimmie Durkin posted a sign: "Don't buy booze if your children need shoes."

The Volstead Act (1919) spelled out the exact provisions of the Prohibition Amendment. It prohibited all beverages containing more than 0.5 percent alcohol, which, by that definition, certainly included wine. The law did not forbid the *possession* of intoxicating beverages, though. In other words, in a transaction between a bootlegger and a customer, only the bootlegger would be subject to prosecution. This immunity from prosecution for possession resulted in massive sales of wine during the period just prior to Prohibition, as consumers stocked their own wine cellars in anticipation of scarcity. Furthermore, the Volstead Act made exceptions for home winemakers who could produce up to 200 gallons of "fruit juices" per year for home consumption. Other exemptions were for the commercial manufacture of wine for medicinal purposes and for sacramental use in Christian and Jewish worship. Permits to make and sell wine under these exemptions were complicated to obtain and the profits were small. Although many wineries went out of business, some became creative in marketing to the home wine-making enterprises. They produced juice concentrate and winebricks, which consisted of whole grapes pressed into a solid form that were sold with yeast tablets. Because the demand for grapes to produce homemade wine increased, many vineyards were planted with grapes that looked appealing and would transport well. Unfortunately, they weren't the best wine-producing grapes and following the repeal of Prohibition, most of these vineyards had to be replanted.

Prohibition did not successfully accomplish what the Prohibitionists had intended. Alcohol consumption actually *increased* following the passage of the Volstead Act. It was noted by many that, in retrospect, it did not create a nation of teetotallers, but rather a nation of lawbreakers. Nevertheless, National Prohibition remained in effect for 13 years, being repealed in 1933 by the passage of the Twenty-first Amendment. Winemakers that had survived Prohibition, and new ones that soon developed, found a pent up demand for their products.

The Worship of Bacchus, **or the drinking customs of society, by the British artist George Cruikshank, who created this drawing in the 1860s. Cruikshank was a devoted teetotaller who hoped to convey his perspective and beliefs about the evils of alcohol and its destructiveness on society, and initiate reform of what he believed was the principal social ill of Victorian Britain. He saw alcohol as the cause of crime, social and family dysfunction, and ill health. In this work of art, he illustrated every aspect of 19th century British society in which alcohol was involved, including the British colonists foisting alcohol on non-drinking cultures. It includes a dense network of vignettes, ranging from mild, apparently innocuous drinking scenes at the bottom of the picture, to images of murder, execution and madness at the top.** *(Archival print, Library of Congress)*

This engraving by Johan Zoffany, titled *Plundering the King's Cellar,* depicts events in Paris during the French Revolution. *(Archival engraving, Library of Congress)*

The radical revolutionaries (the Sanscullotes) stormed the Tuileries Palace of King Louis XVI on August 10, 1792, imprisoned the king and his family, and occupied the palace. This engraving depicts the imagined scene outside the king's cellar during the aftermath. The following information regarding the detail of the engraving is taken from the Library of Congress description. In the midst of the ensuing mayhem, the central figure, a Sansculotte reminiscent of Bernìni's *David,* drags a basket containing bottles of wine. In the lower right corner, a Jew is bartering with a woman for an article of clothing stripped from a slain Swiss guard. In the center foreground, an aristocratic woman is about to be stabbed by two *poissardes* (fishwives). In the general mayhem on the left, a former National guardsman, whose allegiance to the Sansculottes is indicated by his lack of trousers, guzzles wine, while another man pours wine into the mouth of a slain Swiss guard, unaware that two black women are picking his pockets. Behind them and at the center of the engraving, severed heads have been hoisted up on pikes. At the center, a man on a ladder and others above him are defacing the shield displaying the coat of arms over the cellar entrance. Beneath the roof at the right, two men hang a clergyman from a lamp support, while other murderous acts are taking place at his feet.

Temperance

Liquor and spirits were used heavily in the 19th century for a number of reasons. Prior to the development of our modern water-safety standards and purification processes, potable water was scarce in many urban areas. Alcohol was cheap, relatively easy to produce and, by the nature of its composition, sanitary to drink. Also, alcohol was thought to supply energy for hard physical labor and to warm the body during cold northern winters. It was also widely accepted in the medical community as an anesthetic and analgesic. No other substance was as cheap or as readily available to ease pain or soothe the mind.

The production and use of alcoholic beverages rose rapidly during the Civil War due to the large number of wounded and the stress of the times. Following the prosperous postwar period, alcohol use remained the same, but the abuses were no longer covered up by the violence and hardships of the war. Consequently, Americans began experiencing an era of alcohol abuse.

As the nation expanded, the number of saloons began to increase in most American towns and cities, far exceeding the ratio of churches per capita. These early American saloons were exclusively male institutions. Alcohol began to be seen as being responsible for the evils of the communities, and was creating a nation of drunks. The drunkard's reputation as a wife beater, child abuser, and irresponsible provider was well established.

During this era, women had virtually no rights, but were considered the guardians of morality who presided over the spiritual and physical maintenance of hearth and home. As alcohol abuse began affecting their daily lives, through necessity, many women assumed the duty of converting the males of their households from drinking. This soon moved into the public realm. Temperance was seen as a respectable cause, and many middle to upper middle class women began to take public roles in this rapidly growing movement.

This Currier & Ives drawing titled *Woman's Holy War: Grand Charge on the Enemy's Works* was published in 1874. The "woman's holy war" was the 19th century crusade for temperance and prohibition, whose advocates were predominantly clergymen and women. Here a young woman in armor leads a group of similarly garbed women on foot and horseback. With large battle-axes, they shatter barrels of whiskey, gin, rum, wine and other liquors. *(Archival print, Library of Congress)*

162

Members of the Temperance League of Logan, Ohio, singing hymns outside a barroom in support of their cause. This drawing appeared in February 21, 1874 issue of the national weekly *Frank Leslie's Illustrated Newspaper*. *(Archival print, Library of Congress)*

These two photographs were taken by E. W. Kelley in 1907, during the temperance movement. The photo on the left depicting a smiling man pouring a glass of wine is titled "Mr. Peck's smile." The other photo in which the woman is reaching to take the glass away from him is titled "Mr. Peck, you shock me." *(Archival print, Library of Congress)*

This 1906 photo is titled "Harold signs the pledge not to drink another drop."
(Archival print, Library of Congress)

Chapter 13

Wine in Art

No era in art history can compare with that of the mid-14th century to the 18th century, which produced great artists, commonly referred to as "the masters," including Leonardo da Vinci, Michelangelo, Titian, Velazquez, Vermeer, Watteau and Poussin. This age, known as Renaissance and Baroque periods, was alive with creativity and imagination, an era of great beauty in art and culture. Venice was the world's busiest seaport, and Florence was at the heart of magnificent artwork. During this time, wine began to be seen as an object of art. This newly emphasized art subject took many forms – a gift from God, an object of beauty, romance and often times a prop for intoxicated hedonistic rituals or gatherings. Most of all, the early paintings of wine included subjects with an aura of sensuousness and a surrealistic beauty.

The detailed portion of Michelangelo's painting of *The Drunkenness of Noah* (shown above), circa 1511, is one of the ceiling frescoes in the Sistine Chapel.

Detail of Nicolas Poussin's painting *Midas and Bacchus,* circa 1624. This is one of Poussin's early works, which he painted during his first years in Rome.

The depicted subject was taken from Ovid's *Metamorphosis*, in which the Phrygian King Midas of Greek legend guides Silenus, who had lost his way, back to Bacchus. This scene shows Midas (in the blue toga) penitently posed before Bacchus, while the drunken Silenus, holding an empty pitcher of wine, reclines in the background. For his good deed of returning Silenus to Bacchus, Midas is to be rewarded with a wish of his choice. His wish was that everything he touched would turn to gold. He soon realized his mistake and, half starved because even his food turns to gold, he begged Bacchus to release him from the fateful gift, the curse of the Golden Touch. Bacchus directed him to wash at the source of the Pactolus River in Lydia to remove the curse. The Pactolus became known for its gold-bearing properties, which according to legend came from Midas when he followed Bacchus's order to wash in the river.

Bacchanal of the Andrians (1518-19) by Titian (Tiziano Vecellio). The Bacchanalia was the ancient Roman religious festival in honor of Bacchus, the god of wine, but became an occasion for drunken, sexually immoral festivities that was finally forbidden by law.

The Feast of Bacchus (1629) by Diego Velazquez, also referred to as *Bacchus Crowning a Drunk,* depicts a mischievous young Bacchus, the god of wine.

A restored detail from Leonardo da Vinci's *The Last Supper* shows Christ with bread and wine. There are a number of paintings about the life of Jesus depicting his involvement with wine. (Note: da Vinci pictures Christ drinking wine from a rocks glass.) However, the main theme in the Bible in regards to drinking wine emphasizes moderation. *(Detail taken from Leonardo da Vinci's Last Supper)*

The Girl With a Wine Glass (1659-60) by Jan Vermeer, shows a man courting a girl and serving her a glass of wine. The art during this time strayed from the religious, mythological and allegorical subjects common to the art of the Renaissance and Baroque periods, preferring instead the realism of everyday life.

The subject is enjoying a glass of wine in this painting titled *The Last Day at Home*, by American painter James Abbott McNeill Whistler. Whistler was born in Lowell, Massachusetts, the son of a railroad engineer. Throughout his life he pretended to be a Southern gentleman, as he invented his life and created an air of sophistication that accompanied him his entire life. Whistler is best known for his painting *Whistler's Mother*, even though it is not considered his best work.

Whistler's birthplace, Whistler House, is now a museum in Lowell. The museum was established in 1908 as the permanent home of the Lowell Art Association, which owns and operates it as an historic site. Built in 1823, the Whistler House presents the richness of the history and the art of Lowell.

Breton Serving Girl (1896) by Henri Matisse (who lived with an illiterate servant girl by whom he had five children).

The great art of the 20th century was dominated by two artists: Henri Matisse and Pablo Picasso. Matisse began painting during a convalescence from an illness, and, in 1891, he moved to Paris to study art. Matisse became an accomplished painter, sculptor and graphic designer, and one of the most influential artists of the 1900s. He was the leader of the Fauves, a group of artists whose style emphasized intense color and vigorous brush strokes.

Still Life with Grapes and Pomegranates (1763) by Jean Baptiste Simeon Chardin

Interior of a Restaurant (1887) by Vincent Van Gogh. Throughout most European countries, tables are set with wine rather than water glasses.

Luncheon of the Boating Party (1881) by Pierre-Auguste Renoir

Bar of the Folies-Bergeres (1882) by Edouard Manet

Lazy Afternoon in the Napa Valley by **Stephen Charles Shortridge**

Stephen and Cathy Shortridge at their art gallery, The Painter's Chair, in downtown Coeur d'Alene, which represents over 30 prominent artists. Stephen himself is also a successful contemporary Romantic Impressionist artist. He may be more well known, however, by his career as an actor. In the 1970s and 1980s, he built an enviable career appearing in such popular television series as *Welcome Back Kotter* and *The Love Boat,* and was part of the original cast on the CBS daytime soap opera *The Bold and the Beautiful,* in which he played the role of David Reed. He also co-starred with Debbie Reynolds on the ABC show *Aloha Paradise.* In addition, he worked regularly as a model and appeared in over 50 television commercials.

Petrus and White Rose, by Rino Gonzalez,
signed and numbered from limited edition of 100

An Evening of Romance by Rino Gonzales

In the Garden of My Heart by Rino Gonzales

176

The Village Festival (circa 1929) by Eugene James Tily, an etcher and watercolor painter who began exhibiting his work around 1895. *(Archival photo, Library of Congress)*

The Raven and the Wine by contemporary Spokane artist Tim Lord

Chapter 14

How to Drink Wine
and
Still Go To Heaven

The Five Largest and Most Predominant World
Religions and Their Positions on Alcohol

It is fascinating to explore the various religious attitudes and judgments on wine. There are over 20 major organized religions in the world that believe in and worship God. These religions represent over 4.4 billion of the estimated world population of nearly 6.5 billion. Many of these religions frown on the use of alcohol in any form. The five best known and largest of the world's religions are Christianity, Islam, Hinduism, Buddhism and Judaism. Countless books have been written about each and their underlying beliefs, so the following inclusion of some of the basic precepts is intended to offer but a cursory perspective. For the scope of this book, the primary purpose for even touching on religion is to look at some of the predominant religious attitudes regarding the consumption of alcohol.

Drunkenness

In the United States alone, alcohol is a contributing factor in almost 40 percent of all deaths from motor vehicle accidents. Almost 100,000 people are killed annually due to the effects of alcohol. Alcohol is often the cause of marital and other relationship problems, and also responsible for depression, unemployment, child abuse and, in general, numerous types of family dysfunctions. Alcohol is also associated with most crime; it is involved in almost 70 percent of all murders, 41 percent of assaults, 50 percent of rapes, 60 percent of sex crimes against children and 55 percent of all arrests. The United States spends over $130 billion annually on alcohol-related problems.

Along with the evolution of both mankind and the production of alcohol, drunkenness has always been somewhat of a persistent human experience among a large segment of the world's population. It has been an especially popular and dangerous activity among young adults, where its use among our most naive is especially risky and often devastating. There are few people who have not suffered or witnessed some type of tragedy involving the overindulgence of alcohol. In our country, where there are at least 20 million problem drinkers and millions of others who abuse alcohol, this is almost inevitable.

In most societies and cultures, religions have always served a primary role as the moral and ethical leaders and enforcers of abstinence or moderation in regards to alcohol consumption. A fundamental aspect of the teachings of most religions is to steer followers away from destructive behaviors and lead them along a path that is considered righteous. As such, most of the world's religions have some type of guidelines regarding the use of alcohol. Many view wine as a gift from God, but emphasize it should never be abused. Religious attitudes and beliefs vary from culture to culture, and I believe it is beneficial to have knowledge and understanding of other perspectives.

Christianity

"For God so loved the world, that he gave his only begotten Son, that whosoever believeth on him should not perish, ..." John 3:16

The birth of Jesus Christ according to the Gospel of St. Luke 2:15-16.

179

With approximately 2.1 billion believers, Christianity is the world's largest organized religion. It originated in Palestine with its roots in Judaism. It was founded in the 1st century AD from the teachings of Jesus Christ, a Palestinian Jew, and includes vast diverse denominations whose interpretations of Christ's teachings, and their perspectives on alcohol, are wide ranging.

There are 124 countries in the world in which the majority of their populations consider one of the branches of Christianity as their preferred religion. Within a large number of these various divisions of Christianity, the consumption of wine in moderation is considered Biblically acceptable and some churches still use wine in the Holy Sacrament of Communion (many have switched to grape juice instead of wine). However, some of these Christian religions advocate complete abstinence from alcoholic beverages in any form. Pressure from groups such as the Christian Fundamentalists led to the early prohibition movement.

Increase Mather, a prominent Boston minister and the first president of Harvard College, in his 1673 sermon *Woe to Drunkards* put it this way: "Drink is in itself a good creature of God, and to be received with thankfulness, but the abuse of drink is from Satan; the wine is from God, but the drunkard is from the Devil."

The Bible repeatedly addresses the topic of wine, as it does food, physical beauty, money, sex and all of God's gifts. These gifts can all be abused and become instruments of destructive behavior. Throughout the Bible, and in an abundance of ways, wine is celebrated as a special blessing that God has given to man. Clearly, without exception, wine in the Bible was a common drink enjoyed as part of the dining experience. It was also the drink of sacred feasts. During Biblical times, wine was symbolic of divine blessings and a fullness of life.

Almost 3,000 years ago, according to the Bible, God appeared in a dream to King Solomon shortly before he was appointed king of Israel and offered to grant him any request he wished to make. Solomon's request was for an understanding heart to judge his people. According to the Biblical account, because of Solomon's unselfish request, God blessed him with great riches and honor, and made him the wisest man in the world.

During his life, Solomon studied, taught, judged, wrote and took stock of the world as he observed it. Some of his writings contained in the Book of Ecclesiastics addressed the human dilemma of righteousness. In these writings, Solomon concluded: "Everything apart from God is empty, hollow and meaningless." The final conclusion of his writings were to "fear God and obey his commandments, for this is the entire duty of man, for God will judge us for everything we do, including every hidden thing, good or bad." Most importantly, for the purpose of my position, in Solomon's writings, he concluded: "It is for a man to eat well, drink a good glass of wine, accept his position in life, and enjoy his work whatever his job may be, for however the Lord will let him live." Concurrent with the Bible's positive portrayal of wine is a stern and unbendable attack on abuse or drunkenness, with unmerciful condemnation.

Islam

"God has told me that you should be humble, that none of you should raise himself above the others and none should treat the others unjustly."
Prophet Muhammad

With 1.2 billion followers, Islam is the world's second largest religion. It was founded in Makkah (commonly known as Mecca) in 622 AD by Muhammad the Prophet, making it the youngest of the major world religions. There are 45 countries in the world in which the majority of the population is Muslim. Muslims hold the belief that the Islamic teachings are the same as those taught by Jesus and the Christian prophets. They believe Muhammad was the last of the prophets, and his role was to formalize and clarify the faith as instructed by God (Allah). The central text of Islam, the Holy Qur'an (also translated as Quran, Koran and Alcoran), is believed by Muslims to be the literal word of God as revealed to Muhammad, over a period of 23 years, by the angel Gabriel.

Perhaps the best summation of the basic underlying concept concerning this faith is the following quote from the Prophet Muhammad's last sermon nearly 1,400 years ago:

> All mankind is from Adam and Eve, an Arab has no superiority over a non-Arab nor a non-Arab has any superiority over an Arab; also a white has no superiority over a black nor a black has any superiority over a white – except by piety and good action. Learn that every Muslim is a brother to every Muslim and that the Muslims

Garden of Allah, circa 1880. *(Archival photo, Library of Congress)*

181

Muslims worshipping at the shrines sacred to Islam in Mecca, Saudi Arabia, circa 1885. *(Archival photo, Library of Congress)*

constitute one brotherhood. Nothing shall be legitimate to a Muslim which belongs to a fellow Muslim unless it was given freely and willingly. Do not therefore do injustice to yourselves. Remember one day you will meet Allah and answer your deeds. So beware: Do not stray from the path of righteousness after I am gone.

The teachings of Islam strictly forbid the consumption of any alcohol, including wine, while on earth. The Prophet Muhammad's directive against the use of alcohol was on the basis that anything, such as intoxication, making one forgetful of God and prayer was harmful.

Hinduism

"Let your aims be common, and your hearts be of one accord, and all of you be of one mind, so you may live well together." Rig Veda Samhita 10.191

Hinduism began in India, but it is unlike the other major religions whose origins began with one individual, marking a definitive point of inception. Although currently recognized as the world's third largest religion, Hinduism is a name given to a family of religions with wide-ranging beliefs and practices that flourish throughout the Indian subcontinent. Some scholars suggest the term "Hinduisms" might be a more apt term, but, as the Rig Veda (1:164:46) states, "Truth is One, but sages call it by many names." Because of the number of religions comprising Hinduism, it is difficult to ascertain the number of followers, but estimates run as high as nearly a billion. Nepal, India, Mauritius and Bali, Indonesia, are all nations whose principal religion is Hinduism.

The origin of Hinduism is difficult to pinpoint, as are the number of followers. Some of the religious and philosophical beliefs associated with this religion are estimated to date back to over 5,000 years. Today, most revere the ancient Vedas as the primary sacred text. Although Hinduism is considered polytheistic, there is a central belief in a supreme God who is present in everything and who manifests in various divine aspects, such as the Goddess Kali and Lord Shiva. Hindus generally believe the purpose of life is to consciously realize a oneness with God and, by so doing, transcend the material plane of existence and reunite the soul (the divine spark within each person) with the infinite spirit of God (*Brahman*). Some basic beliefs include the concepts of karma and reincarnation.

Karma is the spiritual law of cause and effect (or law of balance). Simplistically put, it is the sum of one's thoughts, words, attitudes and behavior, both good and bad, that follows the soul through repeated cycles of birth, life and death (reincarnation). All of what happens in a person's life is believed to be the result of past karma. This belief runs parallel to the Biblical teaching in Galatians 6:7-10 of reaping what you sow. As a person accumulates more good karma, the soul evolves to higher spiritual states. Bad karma keeps one mired in a lower state of consciousness and material existence. The belief in karma is not synonymous with belief in unalterable fate, because a person's karma can be altered by their efforts and God's grace.

Taj Mahal, **India's most famous architectural wonder, means "Crown Palace." It is the most well preserved and architecturally beautiful tomb in the world.** *(Photo, 1993, courtesy Barbara Schaeffer)*

One of the most defining, and contentious, aspects of Hinduism is its strict caste system that determines each person's social standing for life, believed to be the result of the person's karma. Anyone who does not belong to one of the four castes is an outcast, an "untouchable." The highest class are the priests, and the second are the rulers and aristocrats of the society. Next are the landlords and businessmen, after which are the peasants and working class. The caste system, which began in ancient times, is now forbidden by law. However, laws alone have not been enough to abolish the system.

Hinduism and the Use of Wine

Due the complexity of differing beliefs within Hinduism, it is impossible to determine a clear-cut or single perspective regarding the use of alcohol. The Vedas, the ancient Hindu scriptures, forbid drinking alcohol. However, it appears to be an acceptable practice by some Hindus, while to many others, abstinence from alcohol is respected and practiced. In some communities it is considered a minor sin, which can be forgiven by observing *prayaschitta* (a penance or atonement for breaking religious rules) as minor punishment.

Despite some prevailing anti-alcohol attitudes, ancient Indian art forms indicate the manufacture and consumption of various liquors was quite common in at least some circles or communities. The *Kannada Kavyas* (Indian literary masterpieces) contain revealing descriptions of drinking rituals, modes and practices that sound quite realistic. Drinking scenes are also depicted in many sculptures, wall-paintings and inscriptions.

India's New Wine Renaissance

With a growing middle class eager to keep up with international lifestyles, there is an emerging market for wine as its consumption is becoming more openly accepted in India. The spread of a new wine culture is reflected in the Indian wine industry, which posted a 25-30% growth in 2004. In recent years, Indian authorities have issued 70 licenses for wineries, over a dozen of which were for existing wineries, and more licenses are pending. Wine clubs and other related businesses are also opening up in Indian cities. Still, the consumption of wine is relative. The annual average wine consumption in India equals about a teaspoon per person per year, in comparison to major wine drinking countries, like France and Italy, where the per capita consumption rises to approximately 13 gallons per year.

Buddhism

"Teach this triple truth to all: A generous heart, kind speech, and a life of service and compassion are the things which renew humanity." The Buddha

Buddhism is the world's fourth largest organized religion with a following of approximately 350 million people. It was originally founded in India in the sixth century BC by Siddhartha Guatama (the Buddha) and is the major religion in the following 10 countries: Thailand, Cambodia, Mayanmar, Tibet, Bhutan, Mongolia, Sri Lanka, Laos, Vietnam and Japan. The Buddhist movement is open to people of all castes, denying that a person's worth could be judged by the status of their birth.

Siddhartha Gautama was born to a noble ruling family in what is now Nepal and was raised in wealthy circumstances. His early life was full of life's comforts, with high expectations of material success placed on him by his father. Following the wishes of his family, he married at age sixteen. His wife gave birth to a son when Gautama was 29. Shortly after that, coming to a realization that his life was unfulfilled, he began to despise and renounce all self-serving and material comforts. He began a search for some deeper meaning in his life and, in 535 BC, through meditation, Gautama reached enlightenment and assumed the title Buddha.

The Basic Beliefs of Buddhism

Buddhism is an outgrowth of Hinduism and, as such, Buddhists ascribe to many of the same beliefs, such as karma and reincarnation. After many cycles of birth, life and death, if a person can transcend his or her attachments to desire and the self, they can attain *Nirvana*. The Buddhist doctrine, however, is more well defined than that of Hinduism, and is into divided into the following categories: The Three Basic Universal Truths, the Four Noble Truths, the Noble Eightfold Path, and the Five Precepts.

The Three Basic Universal Truths

1. Nothing is Lost in the Universe. Matter is converted into energy, which in turn becomes matter. A dead leaf turns into soil. A seed sprouts and becomes a new plant. Old solar systems disintegrate and become cosmic rays. We are born of our parents, our children are born of us. We are the same as plants, as trees, as other people, as the rain that falls. We are composed of the same matter around us. If we destroy something around us, we destroy ourselves. If we cheat another, we cheat ourselves.

2. Everything Changes. Everything is continuously changing. Life is like a river flowing on and on, ever-changing. Sometimes it flows slowly and sometimes swiftly. It is smooth and gentle in some places, but later, snags and rocks crop up out of nowhere.

3. Law of Cause and Effect. There are continuous changes due to the law of cause and effect (karma), which is the same scientific theory described in current textbooks. (See description in section on Hinduism.)

The Four Noble Truths

1. There is Suffering. Suffering is common to all.
2. Cause of Suffering. We are the cause of our suffering.
3. End of Suffering. Cease doing what causes suffering.
4. Path to end Suffering. Everyone can be enlightened.

The Noble Eightfold Path

The Buddha chose a wheel with eight spokes to represent the Noble Eightfold Path. His teachings reflect the cyclical nature of creation that, like a great wheel, never stops. The central point of the wheel is the only fixed point and symbolizes *Nirvana,* the highest spiritual attainment, in which one's spirit is released from the cycle of birth, life and death.

1. Right View. The right way to think about life is to see the world with wisdom and compassion.
2. Right Thought. We are what we think. Clear and kind thoughts build good, strong character.
3. Right Speech. By speaking kind and helpful words, we are respected and trusted by everyone.
4. Right Conduct. No matter what we say, others know us from the way we behave. Before we criticize others, we should first see ourselves clearly.
5. Right Livelihood. This means choosing a vocation that does not hurt others. The Buddha said, "Do not seek happiness by making others unhappy."
6. Right Effort. A worthwhile life means doing our best at all times and having goodwill toward others. This also means not wasting effort on things that harm ourselves and others.
7. Right Mindfulness. Being aware of our thoughts, words and deeds.
8. Right Concentration. Focus on one thought or object at a time. By doing this, we can be quiet and attain true peace of mind.

The Five Precepts

All religions have some basic principles or guidelines that define what is good conduct and what kind of behavior should be avoided. In Buddhism, the most important principles are the Five Precepts as defined by the Buddha.

1. **No killing**: Respect for life.
2. **No stealing:** Respect for others' property.
3. **No sexual misconduct:** Respect for our pure nature.
4. **No lying**: Respect for honesty.
5. **No intoxicants:** Respect for a clear mind and a healthy body.

Buddhism and the Use of Wine

The last of the Buddha's five precepts clearly states the Buddhists' position on wine, or any alcohol. It is forbidden based on respect for a clear mind and a healthy body. The Buddha's teachings emphasize man's good behavior toward all living things. Part of his injunction may also have been related to concern that alcohol, if abused, could be an underlying cause of violation against many of his other teachings.

A bird's eye view of the Sandamuni Pagoda, which is located in Mandalay, Burma, the last capital of the Myanmar Kings, circa 1889. It was built in 1857 by King Mindon. Mandalay is the commercial center of Burma, with rail, road, river and air links to all parts of the country. The main pagoda is surrounded by the 733 little pagodas each containing a chapter of the Buddhist law engraved on a marble slab. *(Archival photo, Library of Congress)*

Judaism

"Death is merely moving from one home to another. The wise man will spend his main efforts in trying to make his future home the more beautiful one."

Rabbi Menachem Mendel Morgenstern of Tomashov (the Kotzker Rebbe)

**The First Day of Creation
Genesis 1: 1-5**

Judaism is the major religion of one country, Israel, but interestingly, a larger number of Jews live in the United States than in Israel. There are various denominations within Judaism, which has about 15 million followers worldwide.

Judaism originated in Israel around 4,000 years ago and is the oldest religion of the Western world to emphasize a belief in one supreme God. Judaism was founded on the laws and teachings of the Hebrew Bible (the Old Testament), which are contained in the Torah (the central sacred scriptural text of Judaism given by God as a guide to an obedient and holy life). Judaism began with the Exodus, when Moses led an enslaved people (who were descendants of Abraham and the ancestors of today's Jews) out of Egypt and into freedom in the Promised Land (which became the Land of Israel). Escaping the powerful domination of the Egyptian Pharaoh was perceived as a divine act of God. Their freedom from slavery

188

was immediately followed by another decisive act, when God presented Moses with the Ten Commandments. Through these and other unfolding events, they believed God had chosen them as the people through whom he would reveal himself to the world.

Christianity and Islam are both derived from Judaism but differ in many basic beliefs and practices. Both accept the Jewish belief in one God and the religious teachings of the Hebrew Bible. Christianity's point of departure from Judaism was the birth, life and death of Jesus Christ, whom Christians embrace as the long-awaited Messiah anointed by God to fulfill prophesies of the Old Testament. Although Christians and Jews have many of the same fundamental beliefs, the Jews do not believe Jesus to be the Messiah nor do they accept the New Testament as part of their religious scripture.

Moderate Use of Alcohol Has Deep Roots in Judaism

In general, Judaism is less of a creed-based religion and more of a religiously based way of life. As such, symbolic sacred rituals are an integral part of Jewish traditions, and wine is a key component in some of those rituals. In fact, it is the only beverage for which a specific blessing is recited before drinking: "Blessed is God who has created the fruit of the vine." Some Jewish traditions encourage moderate use of alcohol, particularly wine. Judaism also supports the concept that a moderate amount of alcohol on a regular basis is considered good for your health.

There are also several occasions in which drinking wine is an explicit commandment and, thus, the blessing is recited even when wine is just a part of a meal. The two major meals of every Sabbath, Friday evening and Saturday lunch, are introduced with a special blessing of sanctification for the day recited over a cup of wine. The meals of the three pilgrimage festivals and the new year are also structured in the same way. The Passover Seder (Jewish home or community service, including a ceremonial dinner, held on the first evening of Passover) reflects the view of wine as a blessing even more dramatically. Four times during the Seder, there is a requirement to say the blessing over the wine and drink at least the liquid equivalent of an olive. The main theme of the Passover holiday, one of the most important holidays in Judaism, is as a celebration of the Jews' physical freedom from oppression. Each and every ritual performed has deep significance.

The Ten Commandments Given to Moses

The Ten Commandments are God's laws given to the Jewish people. According to the Old Testament, God gave them to Moses on Mount Sinai after He had delivered them from slavery in Egypt. They are as follows (from Revised Standard Version of the Bible, Deuteronomy 5:7-21):

1. **You shall have no other gods before me.**
2. **You shall not make for yourself a graven image ...**

3. You shall not take the name of the Lord your God in vain ...
4. Remember the Sabbath day, to keep it holy ...
5. Honor your father and your mother ...
6. You shall not kill.
7. You shall not commit adultery.
8. You shall not steal.
9. You shall not bear false witness against your neighbor.
10. You shall not covet your neighbor's wife, or his manservant, or his maid servant, or his ox, or his ass, or anything that is your neighbor's.

Conclusion

Religions are often in conflict with each other, and some even espouse violence in some form. Some of the world's most horrific historic events have been carried out by man in the name of God, and hundreds of thousands of people have been slaughtered because of some religious agenda. In my opinion, a good religion is tolerant of faithful followers of God with different perspectives and prohibits harming anyone on the basis of what he or she believes, or fails to believe. Good deeds are the true measure of one's love and respect for God and His creation. I believe that following the Ten Commandments, doing good in all the ways and for all the people I can, and enjoying wine in moderation is a good recipe for a healthy, happy life.

Chapter 15

Bounty of the Harvest
– Types of Grapes and Wine –

Basic and Most Common Wine Varietals

Cabernet Sauvignon: Often called the "king" of red grapes, Cabernet Sauvignon is, along with Merlot, the most notable grape of Bordeaux, and is also grown in other prominent wine-producing regions throughout the world, including the states of California and Washington, Italy, Australia and Chile.

Chardonnay: One of the most popular white grape varietals in the United States and throughout North America, as well as the white grape of the Burgundy region of France.

Gamay: The classic red grape of the Beaujolais region of France, and also grown in California. Gamay possesses an intense fruity, grapey flavor not unlike melted black cherry Jello. The wine is often at its best served slightly chilled.

Gewürztraminer: The world's most prestigious Gewürztraminers come from the Alsace region of France, but the white grape is also grown in most of the same cold climates Riesling is. It has unmistakable flavors often compared to peaches or apricots.

Merlot: This red grape is the most widely planted grape in Bordeaux, and is also grown in most of the same places as Cabernet Sauvignon.

Pinot Blanc: One of the white grapes of the Pinot family that includes Pinot Grigio/Gris (also white) and the red grapes Pinot Noir and Pinot Meunier. California boasts several top producers of Pinot Blanc, though the grape is not widely grown. Pinot Blanc often has flavors similar to Chardonnay, though the wine is generally lighter in body and somewhat more delicate.

Pinot Noir: One of the most renowned red grapes in the world for its supple silky texture and mesmerizing earthy flavors. Pinot Noir, like Riesling, requires a cold climate and in fact, its ancestral home is the cool Burgundy region of France. This grape, which is very difficult to grow and make into good wine, is also grown in Oregon and California but rarely elsewhere.

Riesling: The renowned white grape of Germany, Austria and the Alsace region of France, though it is also popular in Washington State, New York State, and certain parts of California and Australia. It grows best in cooler climates.

Sauvignon Blanc: The famous white grape of the Sancerre region of France, as well as New Zealand. Sauvignon Blanc also grows in Bordeaux. It can tolerate greater heat than many varietals. Sauvignon Blancs are higher in acid and often exhibit 'melon' in the nose and tastes. If grown in too cool a climate, it can develop a grassy character in its aromas. Sauvignon Blanc produces large crops and is a low cost variety.

The Renaud mythical goddess of the American wine vat.

Syrah and Shiraz: The classic red grape of the northern Rhone Valley in France and the leading grape of Australia (where it is known as Shiraz). The Syrah grape is now grown in many parts of California.

Zinfandel: The much loved red grape of California, Zinfandel is grown almost nowhere else in the world. In fact, the grape's history is still a mystery, though scientists think it may be related to a Croatian grape.

As a general rule of thumb, white wines should be allowed to chill in the refrigerator for 30 to 45 minutes, but reds are best at room temperature. Red wines open up and are more flavorful, if they are allowed to "breathe" in the wine glass for 10 to 15 minutes before consuming. Whites, on the other hand, should be opened and poured just prior to serving.

A California wine country road sign.

The Vineyard

Nothing is more important in the wine-making process than the quality of the grapes, and the importance of a vineyard's location cannot be overly emphasized. Soil and climate conditions are the mainstays of success for all vineyards. Grapes can grow in many different kinds of soil, but there must be a certain depth of soil and good drainage. Volcanic soil is believed by many to produce the finest wines.

The climate conditions necessary to grow grapes is partially dependent on the type of grapes. Black or red grapes need a warm climate to ripen fully, and white grapes generally do better in cool climates. The ideal condition is a long growing season with warm days and cool nights. These conditions allow the grapes to ripen slowly. This slow process develops a maximum amount of flavor in the grapes.

In addition to the right geographical and geological locations, the care taken in planting the vines and growing the grapes influences the final product of wine more than any winery manipulations or procedures can ever accomplish. Each step in the process of establishing a vineyard is important not only to speed the vineyard's production but also to ensure its long-term efficiency. Some of the most important steps in establishing a new vineyard include the following: preparing the soil for planting, marking the field, planting the vines, hilling the soil around the vines, controlling the weeds, fertilizing, setting up for irrigation and irrigating, building trellises or staking for the new vines to climb, and installing grow tubes. Grow tubes promote growth by amplifying the amount of helpful sunlight by breaking up the light spectrum. Most importantly, they keep animals such as deer and rabbits from eating the vines.

New grapevines typically will not produce significant yields of fruit until the third or fourth year. Although grapevines can be planted any time of year, planting in the spring is the best time. During the growing season, grapevines thrive in a mild climate with warm days and cool nights.

The vine cycle depends largely upon the region's climate. Typically, in wine country, the vine cycle begins around the first of April. New shoots elongate during April and May, and the vine flowers around mid-May. Tiny berries begin to grow but remain green and hard until about mid-July, when the berries begin to develop color and to soften. The fruit is usually harvested around mid-September, although the harvest date is largely dependent on the variety, the location and the weather. Before the harvest begins, the grapes are tested for sugar content, as this determines the alcoholic content that will result. (The process of converting the grapes to wine is discussed in the following chapter.)

The average life-span of a grapevine is 25 years, but some vines can produce wine grapes for more than 100 years. One grapevine will typically produce three to six bottles of wine per harvest.

***The Grape Harvest* by Andre, circa 1880.** *(Archival painting, Library of Congress)*

Wine Facts

- There are 20 million acres of grapes planted worldwide.
- In terms of the total worldwide acreage planted in fruit crops, grapes rank number one.
- It takes three to four years to harvest a commercial crop from newly planted grape vines.
- There are approximately 5,000 varieties of wine grapes in existence worldwide.
- Most grape juice is clear. The color in red wine comes from the grapeskins.
- There are approximately 400 various species of oak trees in the world. About 20 of these species are used for making oak wine barrels. Only about 5% of each oak tree is suitable for making high grade wine barrels. The average age of an oak tree harvested for use in wine barrels is 170 years.
- The top three states in terms of wine consumption are California, New York and Florida.
- The average cost of the grapes used to produce a $20 bottle of wine is $2.64.
- Old wine almost never turns to vinegar. It spoils by oxidation. Mycoderma bacteria convert ethyl alcohol into acetic acid, thus turning wine into vinegar. However, most incidents of spoiled wine are due to air-induced oxidation of the fruit, not bacterial conversion of alcohol to vinegar.
- As early as 4000 BC, the Egyptians were the first people to use corks as stoppers. One-third of the world's cork forests are located in Portugal, which supplies 85-90% of the cork used in the United States.
- Grapevines cannot reproduce reliably from seed. To cultivate a particular grape variety, grafting (a plant version of cloning) is used.
- Wine has so many organic chemical compounds it is considered more complex than blood serum.
- The slow interaction of oxygen and wine produces the changes noticed in aging wine. It is believed that wine ages more slowly in larger bottles, since there is less oxygen per volume of wine in larger bottles. Rapid oxidation, as occurs with a leaky cork, spoils wine.
- Red wine tends to lighten as it ages, whereas white wine tends to darken.
- Typically, before harvest, the canopy of leaves at the top of the vine is often cut away to increase exposure to the sun and accelerate ripening.
- Americans consume more wine on Thanksgiving than any other day of the year.

• The lip of a red wine glass is sloped inward to capture the aromas of the wine and deliver them to your nose.

• Labels were first put on wine bottles in the early 1700s, but it wasn't until the 1860s that suitable glues were developed to hold them on the bottles.

• In describing wine, the term "hot" refers to a high level of alcohol, leaving a hot, sometimes burning, sensation.

• Market research shows that most people buy a particular wine either because they recognize the brand name or they are attracted by the packaging.

• There is at least one commercial winery in every state of the United States, including Hawaii and Alaska!

• Among the most popular corkscrews are the wing-type, the screwpull and the waiter's corkscrew.

• The Egyptians were the first to make glass containers around 1500 BC.

• The wreck of the *Titanic* holds the oldest wine cellar in the world.

Wine Measurements

The amount of grapes it takes to make a bottle of wine varies widely depending on the type of grapes and the nature of the wine, but consider the following rough approximations:

One grape cluster contains about 75 grapes
One vine contains about 40 grape clusters
Two to three grape clusters equal one glass
About 600 to 800 grapes produce one bottle
One grapevine will produce three to six bottles a year
One acre will produce an average of two to four tons of grapes
A 60-gallon barrel equals 25 cases or 300 bottles or 1,500 five-ounce glasses of wine

Chapter 16

Making Wine: The Art and Science

La Questa Wine Cellar, 240 La Questa Road, Woodside, San Mateo County, California, in 1933. (Archival photo, Library of Congress)

The basic formula for making wine is to let nature run its course. The natural process requires little human intervention. The winemaker's primary role is to embellish, improve and control that process. This chapter offers a brief overview of the primary steps of the wine making process: Harvesting, destemming and crushing, fermenting, clarifying, aging, blending and bottling. The steps for making white wine and red wine are much the same, though some occur at different stages. Fortified and sparkling wines both require additional manipulations by the winemaker and are not covered in this chapter.

Although it can be made from other fruits, grapes are by far the best fruit for making wine. No other fruits can produce enough natural sugar necessary to yield sufficient alcohol levels to preserve the resulting beverage. Other fruits also do not have the requisite acids, esters and tannins to make natural, stable wine on a consistent basis.

The Harvest

To produce fine wine, the grape quality is of paramount importance and they must be harvested at just the right time. A combination of science and old-fashioned tasting usually go into determining that time. Winemakers aim for the right balance of flavor, sugar content and acidity level in the grapes. Sugar content is measured to determine the alcohol content of the wine that will be produced, and is key to when the grapes should be harvested. Underripe grapes tend to have sugar levels below those necessary for making wine in the normal alcohol range of 11-15% and result in a "green" taste. When the desired degree of ripeness is reached, grapes need to be harvested immediately because the period of time during which they are at their optimum is fleeting. To ensure the right balance of acids and sugars, even the time of day the grapes are picked is important. Sometimes, however, weather conditions dictate when the harvest occurs.

Harvesting can be done mechanically or by hand. However, many estates prefer hand picking, as mechanical harvesters can often be too tough on the grapes and the vineyard. Once the grapes arrive at the winery, reputable winemakers will sort through the grape bunches and cull any rotten or under ripe fruit before crushing.

Destemming and crushing

Removing the stems (in most cases) and gently crushing whole clusters of fresh ripe grapes is traditionally the next step in the wine making process. The process of breaking the skins allows the juice to mix with the yeast, which causes the fermentation that converts the

Grapes arriving at the Basel Cellars winery in Walla Walla, Washington.

A typical California grape picker. Although grapes can be harvested by mechanical means, most are still hand picked. *(Bamonte archival photo from the Anne Anderson collection)*

sugar into alcohol. For thousands of years, grapes were crushed by men and women stomping them with their bare feet in barrels or other crude containers. Today, mechanical crushers replace this time-honored tradition of crushing grapes into what is commonly referred to as *must*. The must is made up of about 80% juice, 16% skins (which contains the wine color pigment) and 4% seeds.

The process of making white wine is different from red at this stage. For white wine, the must is quickly pressed after crushing (or sometimes pressed without crushing) in order to separate the juice from the skins and other solid matter. This prevents the color and tannins from the skins from leaching into the wine. For red wine, the pressing is done after the fermentation process. By allowing the juice and skins to ferment together, the wine gains color, flavor and additional tannins (which affect both flavor and aging characteristics).

Winemakers test the sugar content in the grapes they are crushing, and sometimes wish to add additional sugar to the must to either enhance flavor or raise the alcohol concentration. The act of adding sugar to the must after crushing is called chaptalization. This practice is illegal in California and in southern Europe.

Although the grapes are generally crushed before the fermentation process begins, sometimes winemakers choose to allow fermentation to begin inside uncrushed whole grape clusters, allowing the natural weight of the grapes and the onset of fermentation to burst the skins before pressing the uncrushed clusters.

Dumping a two and one-half ton bin of grapes into the crusher/stemmer (left) and unloading grapes onto a conveyor that will carry the grapes to the crusher/stemmer.

Grapes on the way to the crusher.

Discarded grape stems (shown here), seeds and skins are usually spread in the vineyards as fertilizer.

Fermentation

Following the crush, the must (for reds) or the pressed juice (for whites) is pumped into fermentation containers (most commonly stainless steel vats, or oak casks or barrels). The fermentation process is the key step in wine making. With the aid of native wild yeasts present in the air and other bacteria, the must or juice will naturally begin to ferment within 6-12 hours. However, many winemakers prefer to intervene at this stage and destroy the wild or natural yeasts, which can be unpredictable. By replacing them with cultured yeasts that are more readily controlled, they can better predict or influence the end result. Sulfur dioxide (SO_2) is commonly added to inhibit the growth of native yeasts and bacteria, and keep the must from oxidizing, making the fermentation process more predictable. It also makes the skins more soluble. A certain amount of natural sulfur is created in the wine making process, but if sulfur dioxide is added, U. S. law requires the winery to disclose "contains sulfites" on the bottle label.

Once the fermentation process begins, if left to run its natural course, it will continue to convert the sugar to alcohol until all the sugar is depleted, resulting in a dry wine, or until the alcohol content becomes too high for the yeast to survive. Arresting the fermentation process before all the sugar is converted into alcohol will produce a sweeter wine. Wine-

makers will control the degree of fermentation depending on how sweet or dry they want the resulting wine to be, and have their own laboratories in which to conduct the various tests wines throughout the process. The temperature of the fermenting must is also a critical component in the wine making process, and is closely regulated. Most fermentation containers are fitted with refrigeration jackets or heat exchangers that enable winemakers to maintain the proper temperature.

Winemaker Dawne Sacchetti in the lab of Chateau Diana Winery near Healdsburg, Calif.

During red wine fermentation, the solids (skins and seeds) in the mixture float to the top (referred to as the cap). Once or twice a day, the juice is pumped over the cap, or the cap is punched down into the juice, or the mixture is stirred by other mechanical means. This keeps the juice in contact with the grapeskins, which contain the color and much of the flavor. When the liquid reaches the desired flavor and color (usually in two to five days), the mixture is pumped into a press to remove the solid matter (*pomace*). The wine that flows freely from the press, called free-run (*vin de goutte),* is of higher quality. The rest of the mixture is then pressed to extract any remaining juice (*vin de presse*), which is usually dark and tannic. The liquid is then pumped into clean containers (usually stainless steel vats or oak casks) where the fermentation process is completed. A secondary fermentation often (but not always) takes place, called malolactic fermentation. It is sometimes avoided with white wines, and can be controlled by modern technology. Wine will generally stabilize and become softer and fuller during this process.

The fermentation process can take anywhere from ten days to a month or more. Due to the total sugar content of the must, the resulting level of alcohol in a wine will vary from one locale to the next. An alcohol level of 10% in cool climates versus a high of 15% in warmer areas is considered normal.

An early wine press. *(Archival painting, Library of Congress)*

At left is a large volume tank used to press the grape skins. There are several different types of presses used in the wine industry today. Some of the more popular ones are the screw, membrane/bladder, moving head, and basket presses. The basket press has a piston that pushes the fruit down in a cylinder. The moving head press is similar to the basket press except it presses horizontally instead of vertically.

205

Stainless steel rotary fermenters keep the fermenting juice for red wine in contact with the skins, which produce the color and much of the flavor.

Insulated stainless steel tanks with cooling jackets.

Clarification and Aging

Once fermentation is finished, the next step is to remove any particulate matter that may cause crystals or cloudiness. Clarification is achieved through a number of methods, which are similar for both white and red wines, but may occur at different stages. The juice used to make white wines is often clarified prior to fermenting, whereas for reds, it can be done at the end of the fermentation process or after it has aged.

As wine ages, much of the insoluble matter, including the yeast, settles to the bottom. The

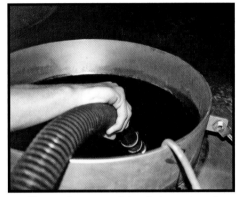

Pumping a red tank to extract color and flavors.

oldest clarification technique, called *racking*, is the process of siphoning the wine from the container, leaving the sediment (called *lees*) in the bottom of the fermenting tank. This may be done once or several times during the maturation period. Depending on the type of wine and the desired outcome, racking may be done before or after the wine is aged. Centrifugation is an alternative means of separating solids and liquids that involves spinning at high speeds. This operation requires careful control to avoid undue oxidation or loss of alcohol.

A cold stabilization process, if used, is most likely applied in the making of white wines, and is strictly a matter of esthetics. Grape juice contains an abundance of malic and tartaric acids, which become less soluble in the presence of alcohol and can combine with calcium and potassium to form crystals. If the secondary fermentation process (malolactic fermentation) occurs, the malic acid will be converted to lactic acid, but the tartaric acid in combination with potassium can form crystals. Although the crystals are harmless (and often processed into the cream of tartar used for cooking), uninformed consumers may become alarmed at what appears to be pieces of glass in their wine. Because of the appearance, these crystals are called "wine diamonds." Cold stabilization is accomplished by allowing the wine to warm to room temperature, then chilling to about 40° F, forcing the tartaric acid to crystallize. The wine is then separated from the crystallized substance, usually by racking.

Pump and filter.

Filtering and fining may also be done to further clarify and stabilize wine, as well as to refine the taste. These processes are used especially with white wines where clarity is of more importance and because whites often contain more residual sugar than reds, which can cause a cloudiness. Filters can range from coarse ones that catch only large solids to sterile filter pads that strip wine of all life. Diatomaceous earth filters are gentle and work on a sieve principle, as do micron pads, which filter out extremely small particles, bacteria and yeast cells. The fining method involves the use of either physical or chemical agents that cause small suspended particles to precipitate out of the wine and,

along with the agent, settle to the bottom. Fining agents, such as egg whites, milk, gelatin, casein and natural clay, are heavier than both water and alcohol and do not dissolve in either. This process may be followed by either racking or filtering. Applications of both art and science are at work in the use of these various methods because, along with removing unwanted particulate matter, some of the desired color or flavors may be removed as well.

Diatomaceous earth filter.

After the clarification processes, the wine can either be bottled or stored in larger volume, typically in stainless steel or ceramic tanks, or large oak casks or barrels. Regardless of the container, the aging process will continue. Oak barrels are the most common and popular way to age wine, especially red, largely because the wine becomes infused with a desirable oak flavor, which will vary with the type of oak used. Beneficial tannins from the wood also leech into the wine.

The average useful life of an oak barrel is roughly five years, and with each use, the oak flavor becomes less pronounced. To release additional oak flavor and extend the useful life of the barrel, winemakers will often carve away a few layers of wood inside the barrel. Sometimes barrels are "toasted" to impart a smoky flavor. As wine ages in barrels, it is generally topped off on a weekly basis to eliminate void air space and thus help prevent the formation of volatile acidity. Wine may be aged in the barrel anywhere from weeks to years, but one to two years is typical.

Barrels of wine leaving Chateau Diana Winery near Healdsburg, California.

Casks of wine at a winery in Sonoma County, California, in 1942. *(Archival photo, Library of Congress)*

A partially assembled oak barrel.

Filling and corking wine bottles at a winery in Sonoma County, California, in 1942. *(Photo by Lee Russell from archival collection, Library of Congress)*

Blending

Between the completion of the fermentation process and the bottling stage, winemakers will often blend wines to perfect the finished product. This is *never* an attempt to turn bad wine into good wine, but to made a good wine even better. Adding good wine to bad wine simply results in bad wine and wasted good wine (but bad wine can be used to make great vinegar). Blending generally doesn't cross the color line; whites are blended with whites, and reds with reds. There is a science to blending, but the winemaker's skill and experience play an important role. Once the desired proportions are reached, the formula is applied on a large scale. The reasons for blending wines from different must batches, varietals, vineyards, casks or barrels, etc. are numerous, but typically are to enhance aroma, improve the color, adjust the sweetness, add or minimize flavors and tastes (such as in the case of too much oak flavor), and to adjust the acidity, alcohol or tannin levels. Rarely are very young wines blended with well-aged wines, as the subtle flavors of aged wine are generally overpowered by the young wine's edge.

Bottling

The last step before the wine leaves the winery is bottling. This stage is gratifying in that it signifies the completion of a long process, but it is also the least exciting part (read "monotonous"). Traditionally, this process was very labor intensive, but modern day equipment has allowed much of it to be automated. Still, the machines, which are noisy and subject to mechanical malfunction, must be manned, and the tasks are very repetitive.

A glimpse of one part of the automated bottling operation at Chateau Diana Winery in the heart of Sonoma County, California, in 2006.

The entire bottling operation is done on a continuous, automated production line with man and machine working together. Sterilization and protecting the wine from undue exposure to oxygen (oxidation can ruin wine) are both of utmost importance at this stage. An inert gas, such as nitrogen or carbon dioxide, is used to purge the sterile bottles of oxygen before being filled with wine (generally filled at an angle to allow the gas to flow out the top). A split second before a stopper, traditionally natural cork, is plunged into the bottle, a vacuum is created to ensure nitrogen is not trapped inside. A plastic or tin capsule is placed over the cork and the labels are applied. If the bottles of wine are to be aged at the winery for a lengthy period, capsuling and labeling may take place at a later date. Otherwise, the bottles are packaged in cases for shipment. Hopefully the wine gods are smiling on the winery, and the last step will be to reap the fruits of their labors.

Empty bottles are purged with nitrogen (blue machine) before being filled from the wine storage tank in the background (far right).

Labeling bottles of wine at a winery in Sonoma County, California, in 1942. *(Photo by Lee Russell from archival collection, Library of Congress)*

Labeling bottles of wine at a winery in Sonoma County, California, in 2006. Colored bottles help to reduce damage from light, which assists in oxidation.

An overview of the bottling line, where the bottles are purged of oxygen, filled with wine from the storage tanks (background, left), stoppered (typically with natural cork stoppers, but see following page), capsuled, labeled and packaged into shipping cartons. The capacity of the stainless steel storage tanks ranges to meet the need of different sized wineries, but the largest can hold up to 250,000 gallons of wine. Mobile truck-mounted bottling lines can be rented, which makes it possible for even small wineries to perform what is called "estate bottling," meaning the winery produced both the grapes and the wine.

Some aspects of wine making will always remain the same, but as technology finds ways to improve on nature's ways, some elements of the processes will change. As indicated throughout this chapter, the equipment and applied science have developed and evolved over the years to control and perfect the final product. Even now, new developments are being made. For instance, a recent innovation is the Foss Winescan Analyzer, which projects a beam of infrared light through the wine or juice and quantifies up to 18 different components, based on the way they absorb the light. To perform the tests with the usual laboratory chemistry would take hours.

This illustration of men corking bottles in Mr. Longworth's cellars near Cincinnati, Ohio, appeared in *Harper's Weekly* on July 24, 1858. *(Archival print, Library of Congress)*

The Controversial Cork

For centuries, natural cork has been used as the primary material for wine bottle stoppers. However, over the last decade, an average loss of 5% (some estimates are even higher) of the bottles of wine produced, to what is called *cork taint,* has motivated winemakers to search for alternatives. Cork taint is caused by a mold (trichloranisole, or TCA for short) that infects natural cork, even the best quality. The mold taints the wine (referred to as *corked*) making it either unappealing or undrinkable, and it only takes a microscopic amount. A single tablespoon is enough to destroy the entire annual U.S. wine production.

Synthetic corks have been used for about a decade, but with mixed results. Although this type of stopper eliminates the risk of cork taint and is less expensive than cork, it also allows more damaging oxidation to occur. In addition, synthetic corks are often harder to remove from the bottle.

Screw caps, especially one known as the Stelvin cap, have met with wide approval in the wine industry. Both problems of cork taint and oxidation are eliminated. Plus, just enough oxygen can penetrate for the wine to continue maturing in the bottle, just as with natural cork but more slowly, which has some advantages. Screw caps also retain the desired levels of sulfur dioxide better than other types and ensure greater consistency in bottled wines. In addition, screw caps are less costly than natural cork stoppers, don't require a capsule and, without the concern of keeping a cork moist, bottles can be stored upright.

But, the wine industry faces a few major obstacles before they will be able to universally adopt screw caps. First of all, there is still some uncertainty as to how quality wines might be affected over a long period of time with this type of closure. Secondly, it will need to overcome the stigma that screw caps are only used for cheap wine. By far the largest hurdle, however, is convincing the consumer. People like the romance and protocol associated with removing the cork and the absolute assurance that, when the wine steward presents the $100 bottle of wine they ordered, the contents are original.

A stripped cork oak tree in Portugal. A third of the world's cork trees are located in Portugal, which is the biggest producer of cork in the world. The Mediterranean supplies 99% of the world's cork. The most important use of the bark from cork trees is for wine bottle stoppers. Between 13-15 billion cork bottle stoppers are produced yearly to supply the international market. A cork oak tree produces cork tissue until it is 150 to 200 years old. It may be stripped for cork 15 to 18 times during its lifetime. *(Photo courtesy Laura and Leon Arksey)*

A stack of cork bark ready to be processed. *(Photo courtesy Laura and Leon Arksey)*

Glossary of Common Wine Terms

The world of wine has a language of its own, especially in regards to wine descriptions, which sometimes border on the absurd. The following is a brief list of some of the commonly used terms.

Acidity: All grapes, and thus all wine, contain natural acids. The acids affect structure, shape and life-span, as they help preserve wine. Good acid levels make a wine crisp and refreshing, supporting the aftertaste. High acid content creates a tart or sour taste.

Appellation: Defines the region where wine grapes are grown.

Aroma: Refers to fragrances in the wine that are characteristic of the grapes. Aromas should be from the grapes, not from additives.

AVA (American Viticultural Area): A defined grape-growing area distinguished by geographical features, climate, soil, elevation, history, etc. that has been given official appellation status by the Bureau of Alcohol, Tobacco and Firearms. Rules may vary widely from region to region.

Balance: The integration of the major components of wine, so none outweighs another.

Barrel fermented: Wine fermented in oak barrels, typically a 55-gallon capacity, rather than neutral containers such as stainless steel. Barrel fermentation requires careful cellar attention, but can contribute to the complexity and flavor of a wine by adding suggestions of spice and vanilla from the interaction of the wine and the wood.

Body: The feeling of a wine's weight in the mouth, such as full-bodied, medium-bodied or light-bodied.

Bouquet: The flavors or fragrances that develop during aging, which become more complex than just the simple smell of the grapes (aroma). If aged in oak barrels, the bouquet will include the smell of the oak (vanilla).

Brix: A measurement of sugar content in grapes, must and wine. A reading of 20° to 25° Brix is the optimum degree of grape ripeness at harvest for the majority of table wines. From those measurements, winemakers can determine the alcoholic content of the wine made from those grapes.

Chaptalization: The practice of adding sugar before or during fermentation to under-ripe grapes to boost the alcohol content of the resulting wine. Forbidden in some areas.

Chewy: Describes full-bodied, sometimes tannic wines.

Clone: The offspring of grape vines that contains the genetic material of the parent.

Complexity: When a wine is at once rich and deep, yet balanced and showing finesse.

Corked (or cork taint): Refers to wine that is tainted by a bacteria that has infected the cork. Corked wine may smell moldy or like a damp cellar.

Cuvée: Wines blended from different vineyards, or even different varieties.

Dry: A wine that has no perceptible sweetness.

Earthy: Wine that has a desirable aroma or slight taste of fresh earth. Pinot Noirs are often described as earthy.

Enology (also oenology): The science and study of wine and wine making.

Estate bottling: Generally means the winery made the wine from its own vineyards.

Fermentation: The process of turning the sugar in the grapes into alcohol. Done by the introduction of yeast into the juice. May be done in barrels or in stainless steel tanks.

Filtering: Solid particles (such as yeast cells) are removed from the wine after fermentation. Some winemakers feel that unfiltered wines are more complex.

Fining: Removes suspended elements from the wine. The fining agent (many times egg whites) falls to the bottom of the tank or barrel taking the suspended elements with it. The elements and fining agent are then removed.

Finish: The taste that remains in the mouth after the wine is swallowed. A really great wine will have a long, complex aftertaste.

Free-run: The wine that flows freely from the press (*vin de goutte*). It is of higher quality.

Fruit bomb: An informal wine term often applied to wines produced from very ripe grapes that emphasize lush fruit flavors combined with soft, low acid structures.

Futures: Wine purchased before it is ready for release, which is delivered at a later date.

Grassy: Aroma or taste of grass or newly mown hay, usually attributed to Sauvignon Blanc.

Herbaceous: Tasting or smelling of herbs; frequently a component of Cabernets and Sauvignon Blancs.

Jeroboam: A large bottle that holds the equivalent of six regular bottles; however, in Champagne, a jeroboam holds four bottles of wine.

Late harvest: Wines made from grapes picked later than normal (and therefore with higher sugar content), usually dessert wines. Most late harvest wines contain some residual sugar.

Lees: Sediment and yeast found in a barrel or tank during and after fermentation. Increasingly, winemakers are using the old technique of aging the wine on the lees to increase complexities in the aromas and flavors. *Sur lie* is the French term for a wine left on the lees.

Legs: The drops of wine that slide down the sides of the glass when it is swirled.

Length: The amount of time a wine's taste and aroma are evident after it has been swallowed.

Maceration: Stirring the grape skins (and sometimes stems) with the wine during the fermentation process in order to extract color, tannin and aroma.

Magnum: A bottle that holds 1.5 liters, the equivalent of two standard size wine bottles.

Malolactic fermentaion: A secondary fermentation used to convert malic acid into a softer lactic acid. Used in most fermentation reds and some whites (predominantly Chardonnay), it adds complexity and softness to reds and imparts a buttery quality to whites.

Meritage: A term coined by California wineries for Bordeaux-style red and white blended wines that often don't meet minimal labeling requirements for varietals. If a winery produces a meritage wine, it is frequently their most expensive blended dry wine.

Methuselah: An extra-large bottle holding 6 liters; the equivalent of eight standard bottles.

Must: The mixture of crushed, chopped or smashed grapes, skins and juice as it comes from the crusher. A term that has been in use for over a thousand years, although winemakers will tell you it is because you "must" do something with it.

Nebuchadnezzar: A giant wine bottle holding the equivalent of 20 standard bottles.

Nose: How a wine smells. Generally, the aroma or bouquet.

Oaky: Describes the aroma or taste character of a wine that has interacted with the oak of a wood barrel, and demonstrate some vanilla-spice-toast character. Most of the world's greatest wines are aged in wooden containers before bottling.

PH: A chemical measurement of the intensity of the acidity in a wine. The lower the pH, the more intense the acid. Low pH wines are better candidates for aging as they are less sensitive to oxidation and have greater resistance to bacteria.

Press wine: Wine made from pressed grapes (as opposed to free-run), which is usually dark and tannic.

Racking: The traditional practice of moving wine from one container to another is essentially decanting on a grand scale. As wine is moved from one barrel to another, the sediment is left behind in the first barrel. It requires more labor, but is less disturbing than filtration.

Rehoboam: A large bottle equivalent to six regular bottles.

Salmanazar: A large bottle which holds the equivalent of 12 regular bottles.

Sulfites: Yeasts produce sulfites during the fermentation process, which are a natural bi-product found in most wine. Sulfites (in small quantities) may be added to wine to guard against spoilage. If added, it must be disclosed on the label.

Tannin: A natural substance in the skins of many fruits, including grapes, that imparts astringency. The high concentration of antioxidants naturally preserves wine from oxidation, and is a primary component in determining the wines structure and aging potential.

Tartrates: Natural and totally harmless crystals from the tartaric acids present in wine, which often form in the cask, in the sediment and on the corks. The presence of these crystals is an indication to experienced tasters that a wine has not been overly processed. Having the appearance of cut glass, they are often referred to as "wine diamonds."

Terroir: Characteristics in wine that reflect the environment in which the grapes were grown. Soil, climate, geography and geology all affect the flavor of the grapes.

Varietal: The type of grape from which the wine is made. Cabernet Sauvignon, Merlot, Zinfandel, Chardonnay, Pinot Noir and Sauvignon Blanc are examples of varietals.

Vintage: Refers to the year the grapes were grown and harvested.

Viniculture: The science of study of grape production for making wine.

Vinifera: Vine species of European origin from which most well know varietals stem.

Vintner: Originally a wine merchant, the term now indicates a wine producer or the proprietor of a winery.

Viticulture: The cultivation of grapes, especially for making wine; when including the production of wine, the proper term is viniculture.

Yeast: Important microorganisms that cause fermentation by converting sugar to alcohol.

Index

A

Alexander grapes 145
Aloha Paradise 174
American wine *(see
    United States*
Anderson, Anne *see*
    Henderson, Anne
Angelo's Ristorante,
    Coeur d'Alene 99-101
Anthony's Homeport
    Restaurant, Spokane 90-91
Anti-Saloon League 159
Astier-Dumas, Monique (Dr.)
    48

B

Bacchus 137, 160, 166-167
barrel fermented 216
Basel Cellars Winery
    106-107, 200
Bayeux Tapestry 141
Biagi, Chris 117
Bible
    perspective on wine 180,
        189
    King David 138
    references to wine
        138-140
    "Song of Solomon" 138
blind wine testing 15-19,
    28-30
Boaz, Perry 117
Bond, William & Marcia 88
Bordeaux wines 106
bouquet 216
British Isles
    wine in the middle ages
        141
    see also England
brix 216
Brix Restaurant & Nightclub,
    Coeur d'Alene 102
Bronco Wine Company 123
Brotherhood Winery 146
Brown, Gov. & Mrs.
    Edmund 155
Brunson, Angelo & Julie
    101
Buddhism 185-187
    Five Precepts 187
    Four Noble Truths 186

Buddhism *(continued)*
    Guatama, Siddhartha
        (the Buddha) 185
    karma 185
    reincarnation 185
    Nirvana 186
    Noble Eightfold Path 186
    Sandamuni Pagoda 187
    Three Basic Universal
        Truths 185-187
    use of wine 187
Burgundy 29

C

Cabernet 123
Cabernet Franc 41
Cabernet Sauvignon 28, 41,
    58, 106, 140, 192
California *see*
    United States, California
Calment, Jeanne 47
cassis
    description of 41
Catawba grapes 145, 147
Cato, Marcus Portius 135
centrifugation 207
champagne 20, 27, 140, 157
champagne sabering 20
Champlin, Lynne
    (Mrs. Philip) 158
chaptalization 202, 216
Chardonnay 28, 29, 123,
    140, 192
    Napa Valley 29
Charles Shaw label 123
Chateau De Baun 115
Chateau Diana Winery 204,
    208, 211-212
Chateau Montelena
    Chardonay 28
Chateau Ste. Michelle
    Winery 151
Chateauneuf du Pape 40
Chenin Blanc 140
Chicago World's Fair 1893
    147
Chirac, Jacques (pres. of
    France) 23
Christianity 159, 178-181
    founding of 180
    Jesus Christ 139, 168,
        179-180

Christianity *(continued)*
    King Solomon 180
    The Bible 180
    use of alcohol 180
Civil War 145, 147
    alcohol use during 162
Cleveland, Derek 20
Clinkerdagger's Restaurant,
    Spokane 87
Cloninger, Glen & Pam 108
Coeur d'Alene, Idaho
    92-93, 99, 102-103, 120
    Coeur d'Alene Inn 98
    Coeur d'Alene Resort
        93-96
        Beverly's 94-96
    Painter's Chair Fine Art
        Gallery 174-175
Coeur d'Alene Lake 103, 108
Coeur d'Alene River 103
Columbia River Valley 150
Columbus, Christopher 141
Columella 135
Compau, Jennifer 10
complexity 216
Concord grapes 147-148
corks 60-62, 65, 197,
    213-215
    advantages 214
    cork taint 65, 214, 216
    growing 197, 215
    processing 215
    synthetic 214
corkage 66-67
corkscrews 198
Cruikshank, George 160
cult wines 46
Currier & Ives 162
cuvée 216

D

Da Vinci, Leonardo 139
Davenport Hotel, Spokane
    10, 67-68, 71, 80
    Isabella Room 84, 86,
        128
    lobby 85
    Marie Antoinette Room 83
    Palm Court Restaurant 85
    Peacock Lounge 85
    Presidential Suite 84

Davenport, Louis M. 67, 80, 82

De Agricultural 135

De Re Rustica 135

decanting the wine 70

Dionysius (Bacchus) 137

Domaine Carneros Winery 116

Domesday Book 141

Donner Memorial State Park 119

E

Edmondson, Josh 97

Egypt
  corkstoppers 197
  early vintners 133
  glass containers 198
  King Tutankhamun 133
  pharaohs 132
  vineyards 132
  wine & religion 133

Elder, Rob 105

Ellison, Curtis (Dr.) 48

enology 216

England 141-142, 160

Erickson, Leif 141

estate bottling 213, 217

etiquette 55-76
  dining 71-73
  examining the wine 62

F

Fernan Lake, Idaho 120

finish 217

Florida *see*
  United States, Florida

flower language 75

fortified wines 199

Foss Winescan Analyzer 213

France 145
  Bordeaux 32, 140
  Burgundy 140
  Champagne area 140
  French Paradox 47-49
  Judgment of Paris 28-30
  King Louis XVI 161
  per capita consumption 185
  Provence 40
  restaurants 21
  Rheims champagne 27

France *(continued)*
  Sansculottes 161
  Tuileries Palace 161
  Vinexpo wine fair 32
  wine exports & imports 21-22, 26-27
  wines in the middle ages 140

Frank Leslie's Illustrated Newspaper 163

Franklin, Benjamin 142

French Paradox 47-49

fruit bomb 217

futures 217

G

Gallo, Ernest 35

Gamay 140, 192

Germany 145
  Rhone Valley
  wines in the middle ages 140-141

Gewürztraminer 192

Golden Eagle Winery 147

Good Life & Longevity Pyramid 52-53

grape juice 133, 141, 147, 197, 202

grapes
  ideal conditions 195

grape varietals 192-194
  Alexander 145
  Burgundy 29
  Cabernet 123
  Cabernet Franc 41
  Cabernet Sauvignon 41, 106, 140, 192
  Catawba 147
  Chardonnay 29, 123, 140, 192
  Chenin Blanc 140
  Concord 147-148
  Gamay 140, 192
  Merlot 41, 58, 123, 140, 192
  Mission 153
  Muscadelle 140
  Niagara 147
  Norton 145, 148
  Pinot Blanc 140, 150, 192
  Riesling 141, 192
  Sauvignon Blanc 123, 140, 192
  Semillon 140

grape varietals (continued)
  Shiraz 194
  Syrah 106, 194
  Zinfandel 112, 194

Greyhound Park & Convention Center, Post Falls, Idaho 17, 19

Grove Street Brokers 110-111, 154

Guatama, Siddhartha (the Buddha) 185

Guigal 1999 Cote-Rotie La Landonne 25

Guigal 1999 Cote-Rotie La Mouline 25

Guigal 1999 Cote-Rotie La Turque 25

H

Hagadone, Duane 93

Haraszthy, Agoston 153

Haraszthy Buena Vista Winery 153

Harrison, Idaho 103

Hayden Lake, Idaho 97-98

Healdsburg, California 110, 112, 114, 154, 208

Henderson, Anne 155-157

Heyburn State Park, Idaho 103

Hinduism 178, 183-184
  karma 183
  reincarnation 183
  Taj Mahal 184
  use of alcohol 184
  Vedas 183

history of wine 132-160
  Egypt 132-133
  Greece 134
  Italy 134-138
  prehistoric 132
  United States 143-160

History of Wine in America 153

Hop Kiln Winery 115

Hot Rod Cafe
  Post Falls, Idaho 104-105

I

Icelandic Sagas 141

Idaho *see*
  United States, Idaho

Idaho Statesman 151

India 183-185
  wine renaissance 185
Indiana *see*
  United States, Indiana
Islam 178, 181-183
  Allah 181
  Holy Quran 181
  Mecca, Saudi Arabia 182
  Muhammed the Prophet 181-183
  use of alcohol 183
Italy 135-138, 185
  Chianti 136
  early wine prices 138
  Frascati vineyards 135
  Montal Pruno New Staggia vineyard 136
  Montzeprimo 136
  Mount Vesuvius 137
  per capita consumption 185
  Pompeii ruins 137-138
  Staggia 136
  Temple of Bosco 135

J

J. de Barth Shorb vineyards 153
Jefferson, Thomas 145
Jesus Christ 139, 168, 179-180
Judaism 159, 178, 180, 188-190
  Moses & the Ten Commandments 188-190
  Old Testament 188-189
  Passover Seder 189
  use of alcohol 189
Judgement of Paris 28-30

K

Kakaviatos, Panos 24
Kelley, E. W. 163
Kelly, Jack 157
Kendall-Jackson 115
Khayyam, Omar 80

L

La Questa Wine Cellar 199
LaJoie 41
Lake Chatcolet, Idaho 103
Lake Erie Grape Belt 147
Last Supper 139
lees 207, 217

"legs" 63, 125, 217
Libarle, Jeff 111
Longworth, Mr. 214
Looff Carrousel 79
Lowell Art Association 170
Luna Restaurant, Spokane 88-89

M

maceration 217
MacNeil, Karen 39
magnum 217
malolactic fermentation 217
Mariposa Grove 118
Matamoras, Mexico 149
Mather, Increase 180
Maverick 157
Mayflower 142, 145
McArthur, Tom 82
Mediterranean diet 50, 52
  health benefits 50-52
meritage 217
Merlot 41, 58, 123, 140, 192
methuselah 217
Michigan *see*
  United States, Michigan
Michigan Grape & Wine Industry Council 148
Michigan State University 148
Middle Bass Island 147
Mill Creek Vineyards & Winery 114
Mission grapes 153
missions 148, 152-153
Missouri *see*
  United States, Missouri
Missouri Wine Advisory Board 148
Missouri's Rhineland 148
Mitterand, Francois (pres. of France) 23
Moet-Hennessey 23
monasteries
  wine in the middle ages 140
Monroe Street Bridge, Spokane 77-78
Mueller, Chris 95
Muhammed the Prophet 181-183
Muscadelle 140
"must" 202, 204, 217

N

Napa Valley, Calif. 28, 30
  Chardonnay 29
  Wine Festival 158
National Wine Queen 155-157
National Wine Week 155-157
nebuchadnezzar 217
New Jersey *see*
  United States, New Jersey
New World
  Newfoundland 141
  Vineland 141
New York *see*
  United States, New York
Niagara grapes 147
North Idaho College 97
Northwest Best Places 89
Northwest Travel Guide 89
Norton grapes 148

O

oaky 217
oenology 216
Ohio *see*
  United States, Ohio
Olmsted Brothers 151
Opsal, Dean 20
Oregon *see*
  United States, Oregon

P

Painter's Chair Fine Art Gallery 174-175
Parker Paradox 42
Parker, Robert 11-12, 22-25, 33, 37, 39-42, 44
  100-point grading system 11-13, 17, 24, 39, 42
  allegiance to French wines 24
  Chevalier of the Order of the Legion of Honor 12, 23
  interviewed 24
  perfect scored wines 25
  publisher of *Wine Advocate* 12
  resumé 12
  wine terminology 40
  Wine & Vine Communication Award 23

Peterson Winery 110, 112-113
phenolic compounds 49
Picasso, Pablo 171
Pinney, Thomas 153
Pinot Blanc 150, 192
Pinot Noir 58, 140, 150, 192
pomace 204
Porch Public House, Hayden Lake, Idaho 97-98
Post Falls, Idaho 104
pouring wine 62
presentation of wine 60
Prial, Frank J. 29
Prohibition 146-153, 159-160

R

racking 207, 208, 218
Raffaini, Rick 112
Raford House Bed & Breakfast 114
rating wine
  five-star rating system 16-17
  100-point grading system 11-13, 17, 24, 39, 42
  Realism in Wine Descriptions 17
Redal, John 98
Redwood Forest 118
Reed, Dawna 10
rehoboam 218
Renaud, Craig (The Wine Rebel) 10, 37, 54, 80-82, 98, 193
  Good Life & Longevity Pyramid 52-53
  Shawna 10, 80-82, 86
  Wine Rebel, The 17, 19-20, 52-53, 80, 105, 108, 112, 120
Renault Winery 146
reserve wines 126
resveratrol 49
Reynolds, Debbie 174
Rhineland of America 147
Rice, William 29
Riesling 141, 192
Rubaiyat 80

S

Sacchetti, Dawne 204
Safer, Morley 48

Saint Francis of Assisi 117
salmanazar 218
Sauvignon Blanc 123, 140, 192
Schaeffer, Barbara 10, 184
Scoring Sheet for Blind Wine Testing 17-18
screw tops/caps 131, 214
  Stelvin cap 214
Semillon 140
Serra, Father Junipero 152-153
serving wine 70
shipwreck wines 130, 198
Shiraz 194
Shortridge, Stephen & Cathy 174
Small Winery Act of 1971 147
smelling wine 63-64
sommelier 58, 68
Southwest Missouri State University 148
sparkling wines 199
Spokane, Washington 10, 67-68, 77-91,155
  Anthony's Restaurant 90-91
  C&C Flour Mill 87
  Clinkerdagger's Restaurant 87
  Davenport Hotel 10, 67-68, 71, 80-86
  Expo '74 79
  Looff Carrousel 79
  Luna Restaurant 88-89
  Riverfront Park 79
Spokane River 79, 90, 98, 103
Spokesman-Review 88-89
St. Francis Winery & Vineyards 117
St. Joe River, Idaho 109
Stag's Leap Cellars 28, 30
Stelvin cap 214
Stimson, Frederick 151
Stone Hill Winery 148
Strachan, Stretch 117
Stancraft wooden boat 98
Syrah 58, 106, 194

T

table setting 71-72
tannins 49, 218

tartrates 218
temperance 162-163
  Temperance League 163
  Woman's Christian Temperance Union 159
terroir 130, 218
Texas *see*
  United States, Texas
The Bold and the Beautiful 174
The Love Boat 174
Thompson, Nikesha 97
Tillman, Gene 98
Time Magazine 52
tipping 73
Todde, Antonio 47
Trader Joe's 124
trophy wines 33
Two Buck Chuck 123-124

U

uncorking wine 60-61, 70, 96, 129
United States
  alcohol-related problems 159-160, 162, 178
  American wine
    wine production 16, 33, 35, 143, 145-155,195-196, 198-200, 202-214
  California
    Chinese laborers 152
    Donner Creek 113
    Donner Lake 119
    Dry Creek Valley 110
    first in wine consumption 197
    Franciscan missions & missionaries 152-153
    gold rush 119
    Healdsburg 110, 112, 114, 154, 208
    Lake County 154
    Mariposa Grove 118
    Mendocino County 154
    Napa County 116, 154
    Napa Valley 28-30, 158
    Native American laborers 153
    Redwood Forest 118
    Russian River Valley 110, 114-115

United States, California
(continued)
  Santa Rosa 115
  Sonoma County 14,
    154, 209-211
  Sonoma Valley 117
  Truckee 119
  wine country 77,
    110-117, 152-155
  wine industry 46,
    152-155
  wine queens 155-158
Constitution
  18th Amendment 160
  21st Amendment 159
Florida 145
  third in wine
    consumption 197
  Univ. of Florida 145
history of wine 141-160
  early wine making 143
  in Early America
    alcoholic beverages
    142
  wine trade 142
Idaho 17, 19, 92-105,
  108-109, 120, 122,
  149, 151
  Clearwater Valley 151
  Snake River Valley 151
  see also
    Coeur d'Alene, Idaho
Indiana 147
  Swiss vintners 147
Michigan
  Grand Traverse Bay 148
  Grape & Wine Industry
    Council 148
  Michigan State Univ.
    148
  vineyards 148
Missouri 148
  European immigrants 148
  Missouri's Rhineland
    148
  Southwest Missouri
    State Univ. 148
  Stone Hill Winery 148
  Wine Advisory Board
    148
New Jersey 146-147
  first vintners 146
  grape juice 147
New York 77, 146, 197

United States, New York,
(continued)
  Brotherhood Winery
    146
  Dutch vines 146
  Finger Lakes 146
  Hudson Valley 146
  Lake Erie 146
  Long Island 146
  second in wine
    consumption 197
  wine country 77
Ohio 147
  Lake Erie vineyards 147
  Ohio River vineyards
    147
Oregon 149-151
  Rogue River 150
Oregon *(continued)*
  Umpqua River 150
  Willamette River Valley
    150
Texas 148-149
  Franciscan padres 148
  Hill Country 149
Virginia 145
  Virginia Tech 145
  Virginia Wine Growers
    145
Washington 77-92,
  106-107, 121,
  149-151
  Basel Cellars Winery
    106-107
  Cascade Range 149-150
  Chateau Ste. Michelle
    Winery 151
  Columbia River Basin
    150
  Columbia Valley 150
  Fort Vancouver 150
  Spokane *see*
    Spokane, Washington
  Walla Walla 106, 150
  Woodinville 151
  Yakima Valley 150
University Bordeaux 47
University of Florida 145

V

varietals *see under*
  grape varietals
vin de goutte 204
vin de presse 204

Vinexpo, wine fair 32
vineyards 132, 1134, 136,
  138, 141
  grapevine cycles 196
  grapevine life-span 196
  harvesting 196, 200
  irrigation 195
  planting 195
  soil & climate 195
Virginia *see*
  United States, Virginia
Virginia Tech 145
Virginia Wine Growers
  Advisory Board 145
viticulture 132, 135, 141,
  143, 145-154, 195-197, 218
Vitis vinifera 132, 143, 151
Volstead Act (1919) 159-160

W

Walla Walla, Wash. 106
Walla Walla Valley 106
Washington *see*
  United States, Washington
Welch, Charles E. 147
Welch, Thomas B. (Dr.) 147
Welch's Grape Juice Co. 147
Welcome Back Cotter 174
Whistler, James Abbott
  McNeill 170
Whitman, Marcus & Narcissa
  106
William the Conqueror 141
wine
  100-scored wines 25
  5-star rating system 16-17
  aging 128, 207
  blind wine testing 35, 39
  boxed 131
  "breathing" 65, 129, 194
  clarification 207-208
  decanting 70
  effect of sun & light 124
  etiquette 55, 59-70
  examining 62
  glasses 129
  health benefits 47-49, 129
  imports & exports
    21-22, 26-27
  "legs" 63, 125, 217
  middle ages 140
  moisture for storing 124
  old vs. new 124
  pouring 62

wine *(continued)*
pricing 11, 15, 32, 35,
  39, 123-124
production 16, 33, 35, 143,
  145-155, 195-196,
  198-200, 202-214
ratings 33
reserve wines 125
screw tops/caps 131, 214
served with food 131
serving 70
shipwreck wines 130, 198
smelling 63-64
sulfites 204, 218
tasting wine 65,
  125-127
temperature 69, 128, 194
terminology 12-13, 27-40
  43-45, 216-218
tourism 145-146, 148,
  151-152
uncorking the bottle
  60-61, 70
Wine Advocate 11-12
wine and pregnancy 49
Wine Bible, The 39
wine bottles
  jeroboam 217
  magnum 217
  methuselah 217
  nebuchadnezzar 217
  rehoboam 218
  salmanazar 218
wine brokers 10, 35-36
Wine Business Monthly 152
wine diamonds 207, 218
wine glasses 62-63, 74, 129
wine in art
  Andre
    The Grape Harvest 196
  Chardin, Jean Baptiste
    *Still Life with Grapes
      & Pomegranates* 172
  Da Vinci, Leonardo
    The Last Supper 168
  Gonzales, Rino
    An Evening of Romance
      176
    *In the Garden of My
      Heart* 176

wine in art *(continued)*
    Petrus and White Rose
      175
  Lord, Tim
    The Raven and the Wine
      177
  Manet, Edouard
    *Bar of the Folies-
      Bergeres* 173
  Matisse, Henri
    Breton Serving Girl 171
  Michelangelo
    *The Drunkenness of
      Noah* 163
  Ovid
    Metamorphosis 166
  Poussin, Nicolas
    Midas and Bacchus 164
  Renoir, Pierre-Auguste
    *Luncheon of the
      Boating Party* 173
  Shortridge, Stephen
    Charles
    *Lazy Afternoon in the
      Napa Valley* 174
  Tily, Eugene James
    The Village Festival 177
  Titian
    *Bacchanal of the
      Andrians* 167
  VanGogh, Vincent
    *Interior of a
      Restaurant* 172
  Velasquez, Diego
    The Feast of Bacchus
      167
  Vermeer, Jan
    *The Girl With a Wine
      Glass* 169
  Whistler, James
    The Last Day at Home
      170
Wine International 24
wine making 199-215
  aging process 207-208
  blending 153, 210
  bottling 210-213
  centrifugation 207
  chaptalization 202, 216

wine making *(continued)*
  clarification 208
  cold stabilization 207
  containers 204
  crushing 132, 200-203
  destemming 200
  fermentation 202, 204-206
  fertilizers 203
  filtering & fining 207, 217
  filters 196, 207-208
  harvesting 200-201
  labeling 198, 211-212
  lees 207, 217
  "must" 202, 204, 217
  oak barrels 126, 197, 204,
    208-209
  oxidation 197, 204,
    211-212, 214
  pomace 204
  presses 205
  pressing 202
  racking 207, 218
  testing for sugar content
    202, 216
  vin de presse 204
  vin de goutte 204, 217
  "wine diamonds" 207, 218
wine presentation 60
Wine Rebel *see* **Renaud**,
  Craig
Wine Spectator 33
Wine, Stein & Dine benefit
  17, 19
wine steward 58, 60, 68-69
wine tasting 11-19, 65
  protocol 58-59
Woman's Christian
  Temperance Union 159
Worthy, Walt & Karen 80

Y

Yakima Valley, Washington
  150
yeast 200, 204, 218

Z

Zinfandel 112, 194
Zoffany, John 161